T0248056

Psalms of
My People

Psalms of My People

A Story of Black Liberation as Told through Hip-Hop

LENNY DUNCAN

 Broadleaf Books

Minneapolis

PSALMS OF MY PEOPLE
A Story of Black Liberation as Told through Hip-Hop

Library of Congress Cataloging-in-Publication Data

Names: duncan, lenny, author.
Title: Psalms of my people : a story of Black liberation as told through hip-hop / lenny duncan.
Description: Minneapolis : Broadleaf Books, 2024. | Includes bibliographical references.
Identifiers: LCCN 2023010037 (print) | LCCN 2023010038 (ebook) | ISBN 9781506479026 (hardcover) | ISBN 9781506479033 (ebook)
Subjects: LCSH: Rap (Music)—Religious aspects. | Hip-hop—United States. | African Americans—Social conditions.
Classification: LCC ML3921.8.R36 D85 2024 (print) | LCC ML3921.8.R36 (ebook) | DDC 782.421649—dc23/eng/20230414
LC record available at https://lccn.loc.gov/2023010037
LC ebook record available at https://lccn.loc.gov/2023010038

Cover design: Richard Tapp
Interior illustrations: Nzilani Simu

Print ISBN: 978-1-5064-7902-6
eBook ISBN: 978-1-5064-7903-3

Printed in China.

I dedicate this book to all my Black, Queer, and trans elders. You artist of asé, sculptors of Osunmare-infused Ori, and weavers of the great tapestry that is our inheritance. Our place in the tattered and shorn, repatched bolt of the fabric of human history now triumphant.

This book is dedicated to my ancestors and raised elders who watch me with determination and pride. It is their look on me alone that is enough to change my heart, my life, my destiny.

For as the ancestors gaze at us, we are changed, and as we gaze at them, the past becomes present, happening in simultaneity. The question for each surviving successive Black, Queer, and trans generation is what to do with this newfound medium. Render art, weapons, or both?

Contents

One

A Psalm of My People

"[This is] a time ... when something awful is happening to a civilization, when it ceases to produce poets, and, what is even more crucial, when it ceases in any way whatever to believe in the report that only the poets can make."[1]

With these words, Black Queer maestro James Baldwin proposed in his famous talk "The Struggle for the Artist's Integrity" the idea that only poets are the people in any society, in fact in the history of the world, who know the truth about us. Who can tell you what it was like to be alive hundreds or thousands of years ago. He starts like this:

I am not really interested in talking to you as an artist. It seems to me that the artist's struggle for his integrity must be considered as a kind of metaphor for the struggle, which is universal and daily, of all human beings on the face of this globe to get to become human beings. It is not your fault, it is not my fault, that I write. And I never would come before you in the position of a complainant for doing something that I must do. What we might get at this evening, if we are lucky, is what the importance of this effort is. However arrogant this may sound, I want to suggest two propositions. The first one is that the poets (by which I mean all artists) are finally the only people who know the truth about us. Soldiers don't. Statesmen don't. Priests don't. Union leaders don't. Only poets. That's my first proposition. We know about the Oedipus complex not because of Freud but because of a poet who lived in Greece thousands of years ago. And what he said then about what it was like to be alive is still true, in spite of the fact that now we can get to Greece in something like five hours and then it would have taken I don't know how long a time.[2]

What is truth?

These are the words that soothed Pontius Pilate in his murder of Jesus of Nazareth. A murder that gathered priests, statesmen, and skilled workers together to kill a possible God because it might affect the State.

I don't write this to you as an organizer, although I have done that work. I don't write this to you as a priest, although as of this writing I am still an ordained minister in a historically white and mainline Christian denomination. I have done public work resisting the State and its men, but I don't write this with any sort of politico in mind, other than the one developed by this country. This "civilization."

Do things feel civil to you?

I write this a little over two years after the death of George Floyd. White america has decided two years of "solidarity" is enough. They have moved on. White abolitionist partners found reason to leave their trauma-bonded partnership.

Corporations and churches (one and the same if you ask me) have changed their messaging.

All them VPs of diversity and decolonization quit or were gaslit out of their positions.

The true history of enslaved Black peoples and our descendants here in america has been disputed, policed, destroyed, and written by our oppressors. *Psalms of My People* is a poetic liberation narrative history of Black america as told by our prophets: hip-hop artists.

Psalms of My People is my attempt to create a Black sacred cultural artifact, a "thing" that cats pass from pod to pod, from intake to west block, from hallway to hallway, to get it in the hands of someone who heard about it from their friend. An item full of so much Ase[3] while still speaking to the current moment of Black Liberation, by reframing hip-hop as deep cries from the Black collective consciousness and as a map to the entire movement. Hip-hop, and some of its history, will be the lens through which we take this journey. Hip-hop has its own power analysis—just like the Pentateuch, the New Testament, and everything that the intertestaments, from Psalms 82:6 to Revelations 1:14, have to say—that any theologian worth their salt has to take seriously in light of James Cone's work and the events of the last few years.

I'm not supposed to be doing this. I'm not supposed to have anything left in the tank, any more tears, shouts, words, lyrics, or love for my people. You see that's what I think the adversary has been up to over the last ten years. The adversary, of course, is called "white supremacy," but we know it by older names. Babylon. Leviathan. Rome. Empire. Civilization, if you asked John Africa[4] in my neighborhood as a kid.

We have watched it rise and fall so many times we can't imagine a world without having to coil our way through it.

In the last ten years, it has been fully unmasked at the expense of Black america's psyche, this never-ending project of redeeming our "lost white brothers."

In this age, we rightly and truly name it: micro-aggressions, generational redlining, ahistorical "history" books, the entire system of policing, internalized oppression, Christo-fascism, patriarchy, disproportionate uses of force, entire small-town budgets built on harassing and arresting our communities,[5] food apartheid, educational apartheid, a prison-industrial complex working in tandem with a political elite that abandoned us. It is ontology,[6] embedded in our language with "black"-hearted intent; it is disaster capitalism, colonization extermination, chattel slavery, an economic system built on human beings as capital.

But doesn't white supremacy seem like more than that? Doesn't the last ten years feel like more than that?

I name it a supernatural and sentient evil that I believe most of the time white people themselves aren't even aware of. That white supremacy manifests itself in the very way they conceive to construct their communities, worlds, and very reality—a "subtle" form of matter like quicksilver of alchemists of old.

Mercury must have fascinated the alchemist: the way that it moves about in water strangely, clumps together, and changes shape, and if you put your finger on it, it will kill you. It's an almost mesmerizing color and glints off the light. The last ten years in America have been like mercury for Black people.

We may have a linguistic and conceptual "container" for the concept of systemic white supremacy, but it doesn't change how dangerous it is to actually come into contact with.

We have seen for ten years, since the lynching and murder of Trayvon Martin,[7] how america has felt about the children of those who abandoned fields and rakes for rifles and chaos. The Black and brown cargo almost reconstructed into a true melting pot citizen, or rather turned into *subcitizen*, offered almost human status if polite, turned human and fully recognized citizen of this republic, with a few polling tests needed just to be sure.

When we are faced with this sea of barbarity sold as virtue, is it the bullet that cuts through an elder at Bible study in South Carolina that is the most damaging? Or the cumulative effect and avalanche of little moments of hate?

Does it matter what leads to such a narrow road for poor whites to walk in this country that the only turns are success and become a class traitor or to become an armed enforcer of that same caste system that is the only thing that gives them a sense of dignity?

It doesn't matter to me.

We are far too invested in the project of saving white manhood in america, a failed project, like any good project is. The fact that adherents of so-called manhood, or white manhood in particular, often point to a period of our history—hundreds of years ago, when they had unfettered access to slavery, expansion through genocide and settler culture, and those locked outside the then dying European feudal system and its emerging economy based on colonization—and treat it like the "city on the hill" says everything. Looking to the so-called founding fathers might be part of the problem. When you examine with lucidity the period of history they lionize, you see their perverse desires for not just us but the world. I do fervently believe if we of these fated generations, in this time, in this place we call "america," fail to stop fascism here, it will spread the world over.

The "point" radical evil and its now nationalist and fascist adherents are trying to make?

Terror. That's the point. The sweet taste of your terror. The meal of succulents, colonized ayahuasca, paired with peyote tea and your tears. A vision they plant deep in your body's cells through national trauma so you never forget.

That feast is our eventual apathy.

The fear, the pain, the self-doubt, the loss of belief in one's dreams, that's the point of everything that radical evil—called white supremacy in this age and in this empire by many—has done. The loss of kinship with one's own destiny or *Ori*.[8] It allows the rendering of a people in hues too violent to contemplate and in colors too dark for america to ever call its own. It is the energy one feels in a slaughterhouse if you ever have the privilege to see where your food comes from. Most never know the utter fear, disgust, squalor, and filth most of our meals are born in. I write this to you somewhere between Berkeley, California; Seattle, Washington; and the battleground I have called home until recently, Portland, Oregon. This place, and the places I have been the last few years, aren't my home. I lost that. The movement, although fulfilling, isn't my family; they too were put on the altar of my struggles to fight against this creeping laze we are still constructing words for: american fascism. It is slowly spreading like a shadow over everything. It slowly crept into my view as I became mired in the intellectual quicksand that is the thought leader–industrial complex in my pursuit for your applause and in a very naive way to leverage the already present cracks in this world system, as if my elders hadn't tried the same thing. The arrogance of the artist as they just learn to speak, to articulate, as if the same shadow they are voicing so much concern for isn't slowly crawling through them as well. All part and parcel to the long-term effects of living with the cancer that is found in the heart of this country and a cold civil war since 1865 sanctioned by our government.

This infectious dis-*ease* of the mind is the postenlightenment system of measurement we have applied to every facet of our world. Perhaps *whiteness* isn't the right word, but it's close. I start this book in perhaps the most hopeless place I have ever been in my life, and that may be the only spiritual or energetic place or space out of which one can birth a psalm: where hopelessness intermingles with the foolish hopes of a new day dawning. Where the pain of one day washes up on the shores of moments not yet born. Drawn back into the deep unknown by time and history's currents.

Perhaps it is only tears that can speak of the stream of consciousness and righteousness that is the food, the meal, the overflowing cup of hip-hop, hip-hop culture, and the undefinable ontological experience that is Blackness. Blackness is a state of consciousness, a people, a movement, a music, an art, a Divine being chained, freed, and now sitting waiting on the promises of the Creator. It is an intangible cultural heritage of humanity[9] that has been seeded across every continent of this world.

Blackness is the whole reason the dogs of war are screaming for blood in this doomed republic's capital. Doomed is too nice. It is long since dead, its whitewashed tomb dedicated to the memories of slave masters, war criminals, and some of the worst characters in history.

This isn't a book where I'm building a case; there is no cause, no evidence to be presented.

This isn't a book for those who don't believe Black people or our reports. This is the swelling chorus of a thousand African Diaspora Messengers. I would say, "Do not be afraid," but we already know america is.

This book is the shards of glass you left me on Sixty-Second Street as a kid, sharpened, wrapped in the cloth of a thousand marches. This book is "the nice light-skinned one," the articulate one, the one hoping you come close enough to cut your throat with a razor, or allow them to serve you in your great houses just so they can light the fire from the inside. This book is meant to make children write on walls. This book is the screams that rose up in Bed-Stuy as the news broke of Christopher Wallace's fate. This book is a full clip heading for your ligaments. This book is the result of a thousand cats building and destroying on the corners of some street most people have never heard of. This book is the cipher you have never heard of, this book is the song you never considered, this book is the power of a mother who believed. This book is about a father who never left, never was absent, and is tired of you talking shit. This book is the story of our first billionaire and the danger of becoming one of the ones. Or *the* one. This book is about how an empire can corrupt, twist, change, and destroy any of us with money and fame. This book is the story of what happens to the Black artist under the white gaze. How the observer effect makes one wonder: Was the void insane or was I?

This book will flow wildly among first person, antagonist, and third person, *three different perspectives*, and will be littered with periods poetic, profoundly mired by my weird prose, and then right back to some facts and notes, perhaps followed by an autobiographical interlude and then by some theological premise that comes out of absolutely nowhere. It will make exactly no sense.

Just like the Bible to the average reader.

This book is the story of Black women, as is any story of revolution in this country. That's probably why I tended to leave those stories and voices to them. Just figured another light-skinned AMAB could let Black women speak for themselves, but I found several points to show my devotion to their beauty, power, and legacy. This is the love sonnet that I never wrote to them, and yes, we can unpack that later. This book isn't written by an expert, just a fan of emerging beauty.

I'm not sure I should give any more to this american culture. This empire. This prison colony called home. It is enough to survive this country, its prisons, its streets, its academia. Even now, it seems like a mistake to once again declare to the world what I think of it. A Black Queer trans person telling the world how they experience it and using hip-hop as their language, quite frankly, isn't the way to make friends. *Literally anywhere.* No matter which way I tell you this story, as I see it, there aren't great roads ahead for me. It's not the academics, the critics, or even people who read my previous work I am worried about—or the true hip-hop heads out there, although they ain't going to let me slide on shit. No, I'm worried about what I always stress about. Not being a clear enough channel, not being a clean needle when my work hits the record, of being more feedback on the mic than eight bars of wisdom. I'm worried if I try to tell you who Charles 13X is, you will paint him in the same violent hues I have been given to color my people and continue revigorate in the american landscape with my labor, an exotic predator. I'm afraid that a living legend will find this book a very poor attempt to explain how their words are my holy scripture.

But that's the whole premise of this book. That hip-hop is more accurately living scripture in the way theologians use the term than the King James Bible. That it has more authority than the Bible compared with most of the ways, meanings, and frameworks people use the Bible for. That hip-hop is the Holy Spirit at work—for a people, for salvation—and should be listened to closely.

Hip-hop has a theology, an epistemology, and a cosmology.

Hip-hop is an *Orisha*, a Messenger of the Creator. It is, in the most real sense, the voice of God.

This book is the story of the end of ages, civilizations, and an empire. But not of people. We are all watching the slow slide of Babylon, this global interconnected capitalist network of business, war, and oppression. Where others see the point in deconstruction, I am interested in wholesale abandonment of any way we have previously attempted as a culture and people—and by this I mean humanity—to establish contact with the Divine. I am interested in the graffiti in Rome. The politics of the alleyway. The muttered words not captured of someone walking past a beaming boss's face at a factory. The silent promises you make in a classroom when you reject the dominant narrative and are admonished for that shit. But it lights a fire in your heart that still burns to this day. I am interested in decolonial counternarrative building. The only way to decolonize spirituality, religion, or whatever word we are using this week for "esoterica" is through counternarrative building and inherent in counternarrative building is believing people's own self-understanding of themselves and treating their ontological view as real—real as my own self-understanding. In other terms, we are just going to believe Black people in this book.

Specifically, we are going to believe Black artists and treat their words, work, art, and music, as well as the science and mathematics it takes to create this thing called hip-hop, as holy.

That inherently means I have to have enough self-understanding to place myself as a Black trans scholar, writer, activist, and faith leader born in the united states of america. Instead of denying that I have a stake in this story, I have taken the route of Raoul Peck in *Exterminate All the Brutes* when he says "neutrality is not an option" when telling the story of colonization.

What he means as an artist, writer, filmmaker, and historian is the attempt to *remove* yourself from the picture is the crime in and of itself. To remove yourself as a subject when looking at the world is the cold antiseptic table, the awful fluorescent light, the weighing of the heart, and cold detached horror where one does not study but more of the postmortem from the autopsy of a whole people.

Western Enlightenment has deemed as righteous the detached, scientific, and civilized approach to telling our story, and our contribution to the story of humanity. A story told to Black peoples in so many ways: the story of a simple people stolen from their homes and enslaved, whose societies were dead ends that would have eventually been swallowed by "progress" anyway. Progress is, as always, the Band-Aid to cover up the places where the worst twisting of history has occurred.

Better to tell you I am biased. That I am naive, myopic, foolish, or brave enough to declare there wasn't a better representation of what life was like as Black youth in this country at the time of my adolescence than hip-hop.

More importantly, instead of trying to pretend I am unbiased, I will share my unique place in this world, and surf the tide of history that could only create you, me, or hip-hop unabashedly. It gives a sense of integrity through radical honesty and keeps me rooted in the idea of a "diasporic sense of indigeneity."

By this, I mean Black peoples' special relationship with land and land-based practices, that was violently severed through colonization. Then those same peoples are rerooted in a land that screams of its original owners' sorrows and your oppressors' view of the world. That pain by the Black peoples of the americas is uniquely transmuted as "cultural self-defense." Cultural self-defense emerges as art, but before you know it, art becomes life. It's why Cayden, Severin, and people with last names like Worringer or Nealman[10] talk about sixteen bars and sneaker culture.

Life is always more full of mystery, wandering gods, eldritch creatures, beings of old, ancient covenants, battles for the very cosmos, and sacred stories that are happening not in the distant past but here and now.

It's funny how white folks think only the Indigenous had a balanced and powerful relationship with this planet and her environment. It might be because the white imagination believes all the Indigenous of Turtle Island are long dead.

Yet like our Indigenous siblings Black culture not only was fighting for its freedom *the entire time*, but creating whole cosmologies, practices, faiths, and new epistemologies based on the oral traditions of West Africa in particular.

It requires authentic and honest personal spiritual praxis and self-inquiry, problematized by my being someone whose culture, language, homeland, and cosmological system were stolen from them. But a decolonized lens of history and theology can offer us this particularity, without losing our sense of ancestral and cultural connection, even if nebulous and based on generations-old whispers within our family.

Chattel slavery, its still felt consequences and repercussions for the African Diaspora people on the continent of the Americas, is also a theft of world heritage that all society still staggers from.

This book is about that loss to all of humanity politically, economically, and ontologically. America as a country is still punch drunk from the fact it was built on the backs of Black bodies economically, a fact that plays out ontologically within the american collective conscience, in particular the Protestant Christian theological imagination. I believe these sorts of interfaith, intergenerational, and cross-cultural intersections are incredibly relevant since colonialism has removed even the means by which Black and brown peoples the world over would evaluate spiritual value inherent in anything that is now presented to us as esoteric knowledge. When even that category itself is indicative of the problem. Esoteric—meaning hidden, secret, or inner—has been twisted over the years to be everything but that. It now means the wastebasket of modernity. It now means things science and progress have told us to abandon. It now means to stop looking inside unless you want to be labeled a fool.

But the hidden, secret, inner workings of art, the universe, this earth screaming for life—these are our only ways out of the current trajectory we are on as a whole species. There is nowhere else to turn in my opinion. You see, I believe we will win, because we have been left with no other choice. Again, this isn't a hopeful position.

This book is also the grim resignation of having to turn a nation's unwilling eyes toward tomorrow.

Hip-hop is also queerphobic, lost, and, at times, its own worst enemy. It would be hard for me to pretend that some of my heroes haven't made it their personal mission to tell me how I don't belong, how I am an aberration. What can one say to one who is so hurt they don't recognize their own loved ones? I love you, I am you, and that will never be enough?

I can't and won't attempt to repair every breach in this book, but I won't ignore any supremacy

or destruction of the community either. I want
to handle it the same way I wish I was, with the
tenderness that every Black child deserves, every
Black woman, man, queer, gender expansive, and
theybie wonder like me. I want to handle it in a
way that I hope puts me, my body, and my psyche
on the line and not the people. My sincere hope is
that the framing of this work draws attention to
my handling of the material the way it should be.

*But the truth is anytime an artist gives of them-
selves in the way I like to think that I do, **there is
no guarantee they will survive the experience**.* Not
wholly, not with who they were before they started
the journey of self-destruction or the destruction
of the ego while trying to be an open transmit-
ter broadcasting love waves that we can all ride to
a sense of home. This book isn't didactic, but at
times, it will feel like that. This book isn't meant
to be the book on hip-hop. Those books exist and
are in the notes: *so you too can become an expert on
how wrong I am about all this.*[11]

When I was a preteen I had an NDE, or near-
death experience, during a freak out on plant
medicine. I had many of the commonly reported
experiences or parallels of the ancients that 20

percent of people the world over who have experienced an NDE overall have also reported: the sense that the universe is actually an incredibly loving, safe place to exist, that there is a point of "no return." Many report a feeling of being surrounded by dear friends and family if they have any, a sense you are returning home and that with but a step over the threshold, you can go there. Or stay here.

Parallels of the ancients is a term I use to refer to practices that seem to cross continents and are also being practiced sometimes simultaneously by disparate peoples who had little to no contact at the time. A great example of this is ancestor veneration: a practice that happens in really similar ways the world over. In esoterica, the formula is almost exactly the same throughout the African Diaspora, which in turn has spread all over the americas and has become wrapped up in diasporic African Indigenous practice here.

But if one were to walk into almost any esoterica shop and grab a book on Voodoo, Hoodoo, Vodoun, Lucumí (Santería), Espiritismo healing work, even the early medium and new age movement, you would see these echoes of ancestral worship beyond the diaspora of peoples of African descent. Ancestral veneration has been adapted in an almost atypical way in the African Diaspora.

Typically, not normatively—meaning there are a ton of local, lineage, and cultural variations—if one were interested in this sort of thing you would need: a small area or table; images or pictures of a deceased[12] family member from either line of parentage; a candle (typically, but not always, white); some sort of incense or smoke- and scent-producing tool giving wafting, smoky plumes of the ethereal; a cup of water or some sort of drink; perhaps food traditional to land, place, or lineage; a white tablecloth; and some say seven wine glasses full of water.

The form isn't as important as the idea that this nation has ancestral work to do or it may break the world.

This practice in Ifá,[13] for example, is explained theologically by Babá awó Wande Abimbola in the following way:

The following ese Ifá verse emphasizes the role of one's[14] dead parents (representing ancestors) and one's Ikin (sacred palm nuts of divination representing the God's) and one's Ori (Destiny God) in leading humanity to success in life by protecting and supporting one. The ancestors are regarded in this excerpt as humanity's best confidants in times of difficulty.

Òsan ni ò sán pé,
Òru ni ò ru pé
Òkunkun ò kùn pé,
Ò pa bàtà m'ómo lésè péé pèè péé.
A diá fún Báalêjo
Ti ńt'Ikolé orun bò wáyé.
Bá a bá lejo o,
Se b'orun eni là á báá so.
Yóó gbe ó o,
Ikin eni ki i gbe ni í tì.
Yóó gbe ó o,
Ikin eni ki i gbe ni í tì.

Daylight does not keep longer than usual,
Night does not keep longer than usual,

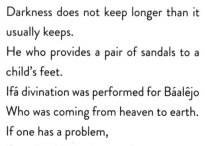

> Darkness does not keep longer than it
> usually keeps.
> He who provides a pair of sandals to a
> child's feet.
> Ifá divination was performed for Báalêjo
> Who was coming from heaven to earth.
> If one has a problem,
> One should take it to one's ancestors.
> He shall protect you,
> One's dead father never fails to protect
> one.
> She shall protect you,
> One's dead mother never fails to pro-
> tect one.
> I shall protect you,
> One's sacred Ifá divination palm nuts
> never fails to protect one.
> He shall protect you,
> One's Ori never fails to protect one.[15]

In this oral text of ese Ifá verse we find
the theological framing and esoteric or hidden
teachings of Ori, which is the Divinity that helps
a soul craft their destiny at the start of one's

incarnation. We also see what I describe as a *metaphysical interaction of the teleological past and its wisdom in the present.*

Put more simply, this interaction is the past engineering a better future through you. By using the wisdom of our ancestors we avoid their mistakes; we are empowered by their ancient struggle against oppression, their fount of wisdom, and the healing they have received. You are no mistake, little Assata child. You come from a long line of warrior queens.

Race traitor abolitionist white queer who got this book in your palms, you think you the first John Brown? You think that you are the first to notice the evil you are a part of?

We are all a product of our ancestors and their work, and we stand on their shoulders. Also in Yoruba cosmology reincarnation happens along bloodlines, meaning your child is *a returned ancestor.*

Yoruba cosmology, and many other nonwhite traditions create a cycle of preparing the earth eternally for our elders, loving them, and caring for a place we will return to.

Ifá points to the "Road of Mystery," which is the journey a soul takes from child, to adult, to elder, to ancestor, to child as returned and honored elder, better known as the cycle of incarnation or, for some, reincarnation.

One tends to care for a world they are returning to and to be welcoming to their own children as ancient elders with lost wisdom from the past.

We "feed" or leave offerings for the ancestors for their assistance, to tap into ancient wisdom that moves beyond time and space.

Hip-hop is ancient wisdom returned, and this book will reflect that. This book will create visual symbols and alchemic language that is truly transmuted in hip-hop, made from the elements of our prophets, warriors, and scientists in stunning visual art.

It will use theopoetics in structures that will defy the white urge for wholeness, parity, and a syllabus. It will challenge me, vex me, and probably piss off a lot of folks everywhere, my special talent from God. It will look, feel, and sound like you are reading Holy Scripture, and that's because you are. Truly beloved, ask yourself, who else has embodied the cries, pain, and secret concrete joys of this land more than the Black peoples of this land in the last fifty years? Whose art? Our art. Whose story is written in the book of life with crimson lines dipped in a well that is more than four hundred years deep? Whose story? Our story. For whom does God bring down empires? Us.

Written in love and liberation,
lenny duncan +

Two

FTP1312

"Fuck the police comin' straight from the underground
A young nigga got it bad 'cause I'm brown
And not the other color so police think
They have the authority to kill a minority."
                                        —N.W.A., "Fuck tha Police"

The first time I heard those words waft out of an Oldsmobile in
West Philly, they were offensive: offensive to the police;
to the State; to my East Coast hip-hop sensibility
firmly planted in fertile dark-brown soil
of dreadlocks and kufis. At that moment,
I was spoon-fed intellectual bars inlaid with historical facts
about our people.

Our history. *Our sacredness*, hinted at on Saturday afternoons in the summertime.

N.W.A. broke onto the scene
by embodying the role of villain, which is how america loves
to portray us.
This is how america loved us.
america wouldn't give us superheroes.

Black people deserved our own supervillains. Our heroes had been taken from us. Maybe only villains of whiteness could survive this place? Villains armed with subversiveness dripping off them like jheri curl juice and with a lil less homophobia. Villains have foibles and brokenness after all, like you. Like me.

america ordered super predators with a side of bass. They got the advent of Afeni's Panther king, and the uprisings in LA had a soundtrack.

White america got their supervillains.

We got redemption,
salvation,

and a few armed enforcers of capitalism
tied up in trunks of cars as visuals
across our young, divine, impressionable minds
and souls.

Wearing this identity as a banner of war, N.W.A.
dared anyone to do battle with them. A mask we
saw several of them drop years later. First for
mainstream appeal, then later to become your
hotep uncle at the bar-b-q.

But in this critical moment for the movement,
they were exactly who they were born to be, using
the tools that were before them. All sacred revo-
lutions start in this way—or continue, depending
on your perspective. It begins when we each, in
our own way, across time and space, step up for
the liberation of humanity. This is the connective tissue from Golgotha to LA, Birmingham to
Osogobo.[1] It is why thousands died in the muck
and mire of Gettysburg, Pennsylvania, why
Mother Jones set foot on the road in the first
place. It is the great game of freedom and rendering a world of evolutionary peace. It is one critical
moment making love to another critical moment

across the expanse of history; thus, it becomes a movement.

N.W.A. artfully transmitted a visceral experience, gripping the nation by its throat and forcing it to bear witness to the experience of Black peoples in this country in real time. *Straight Outta Compton* was and remains a report from the neoplantation that this country had become.

Two years later, after being banned and having their album burned in the streets, they were interviewed. Standing in the waste and decay of white supremacy, Eazy-E and MC Ren gave an interview,[2] but more specifically, they prophesied into the future.

White woman interviewer breathlessly: What's taking place right now?

> MC Ren: The Rodney King trial,
> the verdicts,
> everybody doing what they gotta do
> *to get* justice out here.
>
> [On the screen, an image flashes of a car driving past screaming "FTP!"]

> Eazy-E: *I think somebody should come out with a song called fuck the police.*
> White woman interviewer sardonically: Someone did do that. Two years ago. You did...Before this even happened.
>
> Eazy-E, prophetically: That's because we foreseen
> the future,
> a lot of people didn't like
> the song, now they see ...

The vision they foretold, we have now endured. Videotaped state violence against Black body after Black body. So many Black bodies.

The fires rose in LA from April 29 until May 4, 1992, but they spread to Ferguson, Missouri; Baltimore, Maryland; Portland Oregon; and everywhere the cries of the oppressed were caught on camera. But two years before the first shot was fired in the war, we still fight to this day, before anyone would know the name Rodney King,

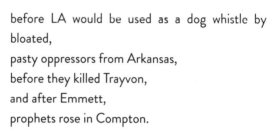

before LA would be used as a dog whistle by bloated,
pasty oppressors from Arkansas,
before they killed Trayvon,
and after Emmett,
prophets rose in Compton.

What would I say of my generation?

We were the Elijahs of our time.

Like Elijah, an entire generation of poor and dis-posed-of Black youth had just begun climbing the mountain that is oppression in america. We waited for a distant God to pass by.

A great wind screeched past us. It blamed us for not having fathers. Our absent fathers, who were held captive by the same wind. Our very present fathers who were stripped of their humanity. God was not in the wind.

Then there was an earthquake. It shook the foun-dations of this empire, and when it was done, his-tory had crumbled. We were told the wreckage of murdered leaders, teachers, prophets, and com-munities left behind in the wake of whiteness's last

generational bloodletting were customary. That this was the path. In fact, we were told, this was the best it had ever been! God was not in the earthquake.

But unlike in Elijah's story, first came the silence, then the fires. The fires of April 26, 1992.

In the silence,
the ancestors had been preparing new warriors of tongue and thought.
In the silence,
in the feeling of having your new sneaks jacked up by a cop who jumps out at you from an unmarked van.

The indignity.
It's not that he slams your face on the wall—scars fade and scrapes heal,
but new white sneaks
are gold.
The final degradation is going to school later and everyone making fun of the scuff mark on your new kicks. Or remembering how long your mom saved up to buy them.

In the silence, God spoke.
God said—**_Fuck. The. Police._**

Olodumare[3] raised up Niggas *With* Attitudes.

"You got an attitude, Boy?"

"Yes, Officer, as a matter of fact, I do."

The Creator, she raised up black-brimmed warriors
with holy amulets infused with the power of millions of the incarcerated,
made of dookie chains and jheri curl drip.
In the silence,
they pronounced a judgment on america.
america which supposed that,
by giving white people a Monday off in January,
they had solved four hundred years of oppression.
These warriors spoke
to the truth
that was plain
to any Black person
in this land.

Our murders were
the holy vestments america bore
on its highest holy holidays.
Our blood had become

its desperate meal.
Our fates,
now tied to this terminal case of Empire.

Fuck the police
and their rough rides.
Fuck the police
and the way they stole your personhood
on the way to school.
Fuck the police
because God had a Jheri Curl,
one hell of a producer,
and a new anthem.

By the time we saw Rodney King beaten for sport;
by the time white america realized
the horror of what they had allowed
to happen, how we, their unwanted and unasked-
for siblings,
were treated; by the time the verdict came,
the one we already knew the result of;
by the time the fires rose,
we had our war cry.

Fuck the police.

Three

Loyalty, Royalty, and Messengers in Our DNA

"And Nazareth gonna plead his case
The reason my power's here on earth
Salute the truth, when the prophet say
I got loyalty, got royalty inside my DNA (this is why I say that hip-hop)
I got loyalty, got royalty inside my DNA (has done more damage to young African Americans)
I live a better life, I'm rollin' several dice, fuck your life (than racism in recent years)"

—Kendrick Lamar, "DNA"

What is inside our blood?
The blood of Black folks that was cast
like dice from their home,
like Moses
pushed out into the river with the barest of
protections set adrift by the teleological, colonial,
and wicked plans for this continent.
What is it that courses through the blood of Black
peoples of this continent?
It is a constant wonder what the stuff inside my
DNA actually consists of.
Is it pure energy from the fabled Garden itself?
Did the angels themselves create a double helix
with inherent resistance that spreads like wings to
protect our people in the face of oppression?
Is it star seeds
running down
my line
that came from alternative versions of this world?
Ones where the church of Europe never conspires
with Spanish Kings to
seize the wealth and property
of Jewish peoples
and never *invents race*

invents race
invents race
invents race
invents race
invents race
invents race

in its attempts to rid itself of anything that won't bow to hegemony?

Maybe inside my DNA is the very embodiment of the concept of the novel. Maybe innovation, invention, and society require more than necessity, oppression, and enemies. Maybe it requires us.

What if the philosopher's stone is inside my DNA? What if the missing element, the catalyst, the needed cosmological ingredient for what the world claims to be is inside my DNA?

When Kendrick dropped, I almost missed it. *When Kendrick dropped, I almost missed it.* When Kendrick dropped, he became a singularity unto himself, the way he bent light around him obscured him from my view. A black hole has an event horizon that can slow down time or speed it up, depending on how close you drift toward its graviton waves.

When Kendrick dropped, I almost missed it. When Kendrick dropped, I felt old. Not yet an elder. Hip-hop is a temporal and spatial paradox, and hundreds of generations can pass you by depending on trajectory, journey, and, of course, where you truly consider home. Thus is all music. All rhythm.

Kendrick has so much intrinsic gravity and weight he brings the distant future to meet the here and now: together creating a wormhole directly to another world, full of possibility, beauty, pain, struggle, the smell of powder in the air. A shell might hit the ground, and the real-time report from Babylon by the Creator's lost children continues on.

Bata drum born in the Fertile Crescent is inside my DNA.

Thus it was my daughter who forced me to shut my mid-'90s sensibility, encyclopedia hip-hop knowledge ass mouth and sit and watch the Grammys. Or the MTV Awards. Or both.

"Daughters can make obnoxious Black Queer seers shut up" is a proverb of the prophet Kendrick.

Would the words *Black* and *Queer* keep their molecular structure under the weight of his music?

Could I be able to see the reflection of my own humanity I had carefully crafted in spite of my own community, even though I paint whole frescos made from a couple of his lines?

It doesn't matter where you stand in any society; when the prophets' words fall on you, the shackles fall, and you look up.

> I got, I got, I got, I got
> Loyalty, got royalty inside my DNA

Kendrick reminds us that generational struggles have generations of traitors. Class traitors. Class traitors who worked with the armed wing of capitalism. I am from the denomination called stop snitching.

On the day that the great horde of *go along to get along motherfuckers*—*aka* the mid-'90s—when my "elders" told me, "Now pull up your pants and turn in your friends like a good lil McGruff," I joined the cult of never let someone duck they Valachi[1] papers.

Stool pigeons. Counter insurgents. Ops. Storytellers. Collaborators. Overseers.

Lotta names when you serve in the Master's house.

By the time we get "DNA," we had lost Prince. We were facing an overt white supremacist on Pennsylvania Ave.

By the time "DNA" came out, the slow descent down the escalator by everyone's favorite orange hobgoblin had begun. It was time to make america white again. It was time to make america 1865 again. It was time to make the church palatable again. *Again.* Make america slum lords again. Make america the Taj Mahal in Atlantic City again. It was time to hide your cute trans clothes in america again. It was time to make america straight again.

It was time to make me afraid again. It was time to destroy hope of a tomorrow again. It was time that I was damned for my DNA again.

By the time DNA came out:

Chad Robertson, 1992–February 15, 2017
Chicago, Illinois
Shot: February 8, 2017, Chicago police officer

Deborah Danner, September 25, 1950–October 18, 2016
The Bronx, New York City, New York
Shot: October 18, 2016, New York City police officers

Alfred Olango, July 29, 1978–September 27, 2016
El Cajon, California
Shot: September 27, 2016, El Cajon police officers

Terence Crutcher, August 16, 1976–September 16, 2016
Tulsa, Oklahoma
Shot: September 16, 2016, Tulsa police officer

Terrence LeDell Sterling, July 31, 1985–September 11, 2016
Washington, DC
Shot: September 11, 2016, Washington Metropolitan police officer

Korryn Gaines, August 24, 1993–August 1, 2016
Randallstown, Maryland
Shot: August 1, 2016, Baltimore County police

Joseph Curtis Mann, 1966–July 11, 2016
Sacramento, California
Shot: July 11, 2016, Sacramento police officers

Philando Castile, July 16, 1983–July 6, 2016
Falcon Heights, Minnesota
Shot: July 6, 2016, St. Anthony police officer

Alton Sterling, June 14, 1979–July 5, 2016
Baton Rouge, Louisiana
Shot: July 5, 2016, Baton Rouge police officers

Bettie "Betty Boo" Jones, 1960–December 26, 2015
Chicago, Illinois
Shot: December 26, 2015, Chicago police officer

Quintonio LeGrier, April 29, 1996–December 26, 2015
Chicago, Illinois
Shot: December 26, 2015, Chicago police officer

Corey Lamar Jones, February 3, 1984–October 18, 2015
Palm Beach Gardens, Florida
Shot: October 18, 2015, Palm Beach Gardens police officer

Jamar O'Neal Clark, May 3, 1991–November 16, 2015
Minneapolis, Minnesota
Shot: November 15, 2015, Minneapolis police officers

Jeremy "Bam Bam" McDole, 1987–September 23, 2015
Wilmington, Delaware
Shot: September 23, 2015, Wilmington police officers

India Kager, June 9, 1988–September 5, 2015
Virginia Beach, Virginia

Shot: September 5, 2015, Virginia Beach police officers

Samuel Vincent DuBose, March 12, 1972–July 19, 2015
Cincinnati, Ohio
Shot: July 19, 2015, University of Cincinnati police officer

Sandra Bland, February 7, 1987–July 13, 2015
Waller County, Texas
Excessive Force/Wrongful Death/Suicide (?): July 10, 2015, Texas state trooper

Brendon K. Glenn, 1986–May 5, 2015
Venice, California
Shot: May 5, 2015, Los Angeles police officer

Freddie Carlos Gray Jr., August 16, 1989–April 19, 2015
Baltimore, Maryland
Brute Force/Spinal Injuries: April 12, 2015, Baltimore City police officers

Walter Lamar Scott, February 9, 1965–April 4, 2015
North Charleston, South Carolina
Shot: April 4, 2015, North Charleston police officer

Eric Courtney Harris, October 10, 1971–April 2, 2015
Tulsa, Oklahoma
Shot: April 2, 2015, Tulsa County reserve deputy

Phillip Gregory White, 1982–March 31, 2015
Vineland, New Jersey
K-9 Mauling/Respiratory Distress: March 31, 2015, Vineland police officers

Mya Shawatza Hall, December 5, 1987–March 30, 2015
Fort Meade, Maryland
Shot: March 30, 2015, National Security Agency police officers

Meagan Hockaday, August 27, 1988–March 28, 2015
Oxnard, California
Shot: March 28, 2015, Oxnard police officer

Tony Terrell Robinson Jr., October 18, 1995–March 6, 2015
Madison, Wisconsin
Shot: March 6, 2015, Madison police officer

Janisha Fonville, March 3, 1994–February 18, 2015
Charlotte, North Carolina
Shot: February 18, 2015, Charlotte-Mecklenburg police officer

Natasha McKenna, January 9, 1978–February 8, 2015
Fairfax County, Virginia
Tasered/Cardiac Arrest: February 3, 2015, Fairfax County sheriff's deputies

Jerame C. Reid, June 8, 1978–December 30, 2014
Bridgeton, New Jersey
Shot: December 30, 2014, Bridgeton police officer

Rumain Brisbon, November 24, 1980–December 2, 2014
Phoenix, Arizona
Shot: December 2, 2014, Phoenix police officer

Tamir Rice, June 15, 2002–November 22, 2014
Cleveland, Ohio
Shot: November 22, 2014, Cleveland police officer

Akai Kareem Gurley, November 12, 1986–November 20, 2014
Brooklyn, New York City, New York
Shot: November 20, 2014, New York City police officer

Tanisha N. Anderson, January 22, 1977–November 13, 2014
Cleveland, Ohio
Physically Restrained/Brute Force: November 13, 2014, Cleveland police officers

Dante Parker, August 14, 1977–August 12, 2014
Victorville, California
Tasered/Excessive Force: August 12, 2014, San Bernardino County sheriff's deputies

Ezell Ford, October 14, 1988–August 11, 2014
Florence, Los Angeles, California
Shot: August 11, 2014, Los Angeles police officers

Michael Brown Jr., May 20, 1996–August 9, 2014
Ferguson, Missouri
Shot: August 9, 2014, Ferguson police officer

John Crawford III, July 29, 1992–August 5, 2014
Beavercreek, Ohio
Shot: August 5, 2014, Beavercreek police officer

Tyree Woodson, July 8, 1976–August 2, 2014
Baltimore, Maryland
Shot: August 2, 2014, Baltimore City police
officer

Eric Garner, September 15, 1970–July 17, 2014
Staten Island, New York
Choke Hold/Suffocated: July 17, 2014, New York
City police officer

**Dontre Hamilton, January 20, 1983–April 30,
2014**
Milwaukee, Wisconsin
Shot: April 30, 2014, Milwaukee police officer

**Victor White III, September 11, 1991–March 3,
2014**
New Iberia, Louisiana
Shot: March 2, 2014, Iberia Parish sheriff's deputy

**Gabriella Monique Nevarez, November 25,
1991–March 2, 2014**
Citrus Heights, California

Shot: March 2, 2014, Citrus Heights police officers

Yvette Smith, December 18, 1966–February 16, 2014
Bastrop County, Texas
Shot: February 16, 2014, Bastrop County sheriff's deputy

McKenzie J. Cochran, August 25, 1988–January 29, 2014
Southfield, Michigan
Pepper Sprayed/Compression Asphyxiation: January 28, 2014, Northland Mall security guards

Jordan Baker, 1988–January 16, 2014
Houston, Texas
Shot: January 16, 2014, off-duty Houston police officer

Andy Lopez, June 2, 2000–October 22, 2013
Santa Rosa, California
Shot: October 22, 2013, Sonoma County sheriff's deputy

Miriam Iris Carey, August 12, 1979–October 3, 2013
Washington, DC

Shot twenty-six times: October 3, 2013, US Secret Service officer

Barrington "BJ" Williams, 1988–September 17, 2013
New York City, New York
Neglect/Disdain/Asthma Attack: September 17, 2013, New York City police officers

Jonathan Ferrell, October 11, 1989–September 14, 2013
Charlotte, North Carolina
Shot: September 14, 2013, Charlotte-Mecklenburg police officer

Carlos Alcis, 1970–August 15, 2013
Brooklyn, New York City
Heart Attack/Neglect: August 15, 2013, New York City police officers

Larry Eugene Jackson Jr., November 29, 1980–July 26, 2013
Austin, Texas
Shot: July 26, 2013, Austin police detective

Kyam Livingston, July 29, 1975–July 21, 2013
New York City, New York

Neglect/Ignored Pleas for Help: July 20–21, 2013, New York City police officers

Clinton R. Allen, September 26, 1987–March 10, 2013
Dallas, Texas
Tasered and Shot: March 10, 2013, Dallas police officer

Kimani "KiKi" Gray, October 19, 1996–March 9, 2013
Brooklyn, New York City, New York
Shot: March 9, 2013, New York police officers

Kayla Moore, April 17, 1971–February 13, 2013
Berkeley, California
Restrained Face-Down Prone: February 12, 2013, Berkeley police officers

Jamaal Moore Sr., 1989–December 15, 2012
Chicago, Illinois
Shot: December 15, 2012, Chicago police officer

Shelly Marie Frey, April 21, 1985–December 6, 2012
Houston, Texas

Shot: December 6, 2012, off-duty Harris County sheriff's deputy

Darnisha Diana Harris, December 11, 1996–December 2, 2012
Breaux Bridge, Louisiana
Shot: December 2, 2012, Breaux Bridge police officer

Timothy Russell, December 9. 1968–November 29, 2012
Cleveland, Ohio
137 Rounds/Shot 23 times: November 29, 2012, Cleveland police officers

Malissa Williams, June 20, 1982–November 29, 2012
Cleveland, Ohio
137 Rounds/Shot 24 times: November 29, 2012, Cleveland police officers

Noel Palanco, November 28, 1989–October 4, 2012
Queens, New York City, New York
Shot: October 4, 2012, New York City police officers

Reynaldo Cuevas, January 6, 1992–September 7, 2012
The Bronx, New York City, New York
Shot: September 7, 2012, New York City police officer

Chavis Carter, 1991–July 28, 2012
Jonesboro, Arkansas
Shot: July 28, 2012, Jonesboro police officer

Alesia Thomas, June 1, 1977–July 22, 2012
Los Angeles, California
Brutal Force/Beaten: July 22, 2012, Los Angeles police officers

Shantel Davis, May 26, 1989–June 14, 2012
New York City, New York
Shot: June 14, 2012, New York City police officer

Sharmel T. Edwards, October 10, 1962–April 21, 2012
Las Vegas, Nevada
Shot: April 21, 2012, Las Vegas police officers

Tamon Robinson, December 21, 1985–April 18, 2012
Brooklyn, New York City, New York

Run Over by Police Car: April 12, 2012, New York City police officers

Ervin Lee Jefferson III, 1994–March 24, 2012
Atlanta, Georgia
Shot: March 24, 2012, Shepperson Security & Escort Services security guards

Kendrec McDade, May 5, 1992–March 24, 2012
Pasadena, California
Shot: March 24, 2012, Pasadena police officers

Rekia Boyd, November 5, 1989–March 21, 2012
Chicago, Illinois
Shot: March 21, 2012, off-duty Chicago police detective

Shereese Francis, 1982–March 15, 2012
Queens, New York City, New York
Suffocated to Death: March 15, 2012, New York City police officers

Jersey K. Green, June 17, 1974–March 12, 2012
Aurora, Illinois
Tasered/Electrocuted: March 12, 2012, Aurora police officers

Wendell James Allen, December 19, 1991–March 7, 2012

New Orleans, Louisiana

Shot: March 7, 2012, New Orleans police officer

Nehemiah Lazar Dillard, July 29, 1982–March 5, 2012

Gainesville, Florida

Tasered/Electrocuted: March 5, 2012, Alachua County sheriff's deputies

Dante' Lamar Price, July 18, 1986–March 1, 2012

Dayton, Ohio

Shot: March 1, 2012, Ranger Security Guards

Raymond Luther Allen Jr., 1978–February 29, 2012

Galveston, Texas

Tasered/Electrocuted: February 27, 2012, Galveston police officers

Johnnie Kamahi Warren, February 26, 1968–February 13, 2012

Dothan, Alabama

Tasered/Electrocuted: December 10, 2012, Houston County (AL) sheriff's deputy

Manual Levi Loggins Jr., February 22, 1980– February 7, 2012
San Clemente, Orange County, California
Shot: February 7, 2012, Orange County sheriff's deputy

Ramarley Graham, April 12, 1993–February 2, 2012
The Bronx, New York City, New York
Shot: February 2, 2012, New York City police officer

Kenneth Chamberlain Sr., April 12, 1943– November 19, 2011
White Plains, New York
Tasered/Electrocuted/Shot: November 19, 2011, White Plains police officers

Alonzo Ashley, June 10, 1982–July 18, 2011
Denver, Colorado
Tasered/Electrocuted: July 18, 2011, Denver police officers

Derek Williams, January 23, 1989–July 6, 2011
Milwaukee, Wisconsin
Blunt Force/Respiratory Distress: July 6, 2011, Milwaukee police officers

Raheim Brown Jr., March 4, 1990–January 22, 2011
Oakland, California
Shot: January 22, 2011, Oakland Unified School District police

Reginald Doucet, June 3, 1985–January 14, 2011
Los Angeles, California
Shot: January 14, 2011, Los Angeles police officer

Derrick Jones, September 30, 1973–November 8, 2010
Oakland, California
Shot: November 8, 2010, Oakland police officers

Danroy "DJ" Henry Jr., October 29, 1990–October 17, 2010
Pleasantville, New York
Shot: October 17, 2020, Pleasantville police officer

Aiyana Mo'Nay Stanley-Jones, July 20, 2002–May 16, 2010
Detroit, Michigan
Shot: May 16, 2010, Detroit police officer

Steven Eugene Washington, September 20, 1982–March 20, 2010
Los Angeles, California
Shot: March 20, 2010, Los Angeles County police

Aaron Campbell, September 7, 1984–January 29, 2010
Portland, Oregon
Shot: January 29, 2010, Portland police officer

Kiwane Carrington, July 14, 1994–October 9, 2009
Champaign, Illinois
Shot: October 9, 2019, Champaign police officer

Victor Steen, November 11, 1991–October 3, 2009
Pensacola, Florida
Tasered/Run over: October 3, 2009, Pensacola police officer

Shem Walker, March 18, 1960–July 11, 2009
Brooklyn, New York
Shot: July 11, 2009, New York City undercover C-94 police officer

Oscar Grant III, February 27, 1986–January 1, 2009
Oakland, California
Shot: January 1, 2009, BART police officer

Tarika Wilson, October 30, 1981–January 4, 2008
Lima, Ohio
Shot January 4, 2008, Lima police officer

DeAunta Terrel Farrow, September 7, 1994–June 22, 2007
West Memphis, Arkansas
Shot: June 22, 2007, West Memphis (AR) police officer

Sean Bell, May 23, 1983–November 25, 2006
Queens, New York City, New York
Shot: November 25, 2006, New York City police officers

Kathryn Johnston, June 26, 1914–November 21, 2006
Atlanta, Georgia
Shot: November 21, 2006, undercover Atlanta police officers

Ronald Curtis Madison, March 1, 1965–September 4, 2005
Danziger Bridge, New Orleans, Louisiana
Shot: September 4, 2005, New Orleans police officers

James B. Brissette Jr., November 6, 1987–September 4, 2005
Danziger Bridge, New Orleans, Louisiana
Shot: September 4, 2005, New Orleans police officers

Henry "Ace" Glover, October 2, 1973–September 2, 2005
New Orleans, Louisiana
Shot: September 2, 2005, New Orleans police officers

Timothy Stansbury Jr., November 16, 1984–January 24, 2004
Brooklyn, New York City, New York
Shot: January 24, 2004, New York City police officer

Ousmane Zongo, 1960–May 22, 2003
New York City, New York

Shot: May 22, 2003, New York City police officer

Alberta Spruill, 1946–May 16, 2003
New York City, New York
Stun Grenade (thrown into her apartment, led to a heart attack): May 16, 2003, New York City police officer

Kendra Sarie James, December 24, 1981–May 5, 2003
Portland, Oregon
Shot: May 5, 2003, Portland police officer

Orlando Barlow, December 29, 1974–February 28, 2003
Las Vegas, Nevada
Shot: February 28, 2003, Las Vegas police officer

Nelson Martinez-Mendez, 1977–August 8, 2001
Bellevue, Washington
Shot: August 8, 2001, Bellevue police officer

Timothy DeWayne Thomas Jr., July 25, 1981–April 7, 2001
Cincinnati, Ohio
Shot: April 7, 2001, Cincinnati police patrolman

Prince Carmen Jones Jr., March 30, 1975–September 1, 2000
Fairfax County, Virginia
Shot: September 1, 2000, Prince George's County police officer

Ronald Beasley, 1964–June 12, 2000
Dellwood, Missouri
Shot: June 12, 2000, Dellwood police officers

Earl Murray, 1964–June 12, 2000
Dellwood, Missouri
Shot: June 12, 2000, Dellwood police officers

Patrick Moses Dorismond, February 28, 1974–March 16, 2000
New York City, New York
Shot: March 16, 2000,
New York City police officer

Malcolm Ferguson, October 31, 1976–March 1, 2000
The Bronx, New York City, New York
Shot: March 1, 2000, New York City police officer[2]

How many names did you skip over just now?
Did I skip over? Did we skip over any names
I mean there is so much: loyalty, got royalty
inside my DNA
How in the fuck can you say: that hip-hop
has done more damage to
young African Americans
than racism in recent years?

What is so precious in our DNA that this much
blood,
this much gore,
this much human life must be snatched?
Cut short.
Who are we to you america?

By the time "DNA" came out,
I wouldn't let anyone question mine.

By the time "DNA" came out,
I was about to launch a church.

By the time you read this,
it may have been years since I have gone to one
voluntarily.

By the time "DNA" came out,
I had mostly written my first book in my head, and
here I am writing in my fourth.
And that me seems
like a stranger.

By the time "DNA" came out,
Tulsa had finally reentered the lexicon of
Black america.
Black Wall Street's erasure was now
old news.

By the time "DNA" came out,
Bible studies were now slaughterhouses,
and the name Clementa Pickney
was well known.

By the time "DNA" came out,
MAGA
was the new order emerging out of midwestern
pride and rusted futures.

By the time "DNA" came out,
Watts, Baltimore, Ferguson, the Twin Cities,
Miracles on Black Friday on the Miracle Mile,

and they started to understand what is inside our DNA.

By the time "DNA" came out,
bus boycotts, assassinations,
and Rev. Officer Sharpton had probably snitched
at least four times.
He didn't recall.

By the time "DNA" came out,
my brother Danny finally got out
before going
back in.

By the time "DNA" came out,
the deadliest occupation in america claimed:
Scott La Rock, 2Pac, Biggie, Paul C, D Boy,
Charizma, Stretch, Seagram, Yaki Kadafi, Fat Pat,
Big L, Freaky Tah, Bugz, DJ Uncle Al, Jam Master
Jay, Sabotage, Camoflauge, Half a Mill, Soulja Slim,
Mac Dre, Blade Icewood, Proof, Big Hawk, VL
Mike, Dolla, Lele, Magnolia Shorty,[3] and more ...

By the time "DNA" came out,
Black america had so many EGOTs

diamond, platinum, triple gold records from us
they forget they destroyed our entire culture for
diamonds, platinum, and gold.

By the time "DNA" came out, we
actually wondered aloud
did Black Lives Matter?

By the time "DNA" came out,
I had come out
to friends
my then wife, and others,
but not the world.

"DNA" dropped
into my life April 18, 2017.
Where were you?

I was in a seminary
in Philadelphia disturbed enough by now
to be publicly asking the question:
Will this republic survive these next few years?
Unaware the answer would take
decades.

What was in my DNA?
Four hundred years of resilience
ancestral rage
that had been honed down
to the sharp sword's edge
that was meeting
the day and the age
inside my DNA.

Four

When East Meets West

"Dear Mama don't cry, your baby boy's doing good
Tell the homies I'm in Heaven and they ain't got hoods
Seen a show with Marvin Gaye last night, it had me
shook
Drinking peppermint Schnapps, with Jackie Wilson, and
Sam Cooke
Then some lady named Billie Holiday,
Sang sitting there kicking it with Malcolm, 'til the
day came"

—2Pac, "Thugz Mansion"

What is home? There are very few roads that lead to peace
and tranquility for a Black artist. Most are forced to embrace

Diaspora in exchange for capitalism and left to ask, where can you hang your hat? Your cloak that you have to wear throughout the world that is intricately covered with the symbols, metaphors, and rough sketches of adornment that are only reflective of white america *thinks* Blackness is.

Where can you take off the mask, the character you have been typecast in? Where breathtaking dawns aren't interrupted by the sound of a child's growling stomach as the dew weighs down roses and shines more lights on the world than the shattered glass of our dreams.

Home. A timeline. A universe. An anomaly.
A paradox of a temporal flavor with spatial impact.
A mirage. A hope.
The weight at the end of the apparently
never-ending
arc of HISstory bending us
toward what this world dares to claim is justice.

Where is home? Where is the Kin-dom come? Where is the throne of all liberation for the caramel brown and black shades of those of us who were brought to these bitter shores? Where is our great chorus in the infinite hosannas being sung to the benign heavenly governments in the mansions, shores, and vineyards of our collective rest?

"need a spot where we can kick it ..."

It is with those words the prince of a Panther Queen—a Queen who had fallen from grace and was taken in by Freeway Ricky's[1] scam, like my father was—gave us the live report from a nexus of possibility. It is my sincere belief that Tupac Shakur is the victim of COINTELPRO. That the fear of one artist, of art, of music, of revolution, being united with the kids suffering on the streets was enough.

The fear that killed Brother Martin.
The fear
that tried to erase this prince's mother from the annals of history.
That has Assata still
in exile.
That murdered Fred
in his home

while the chairman was still
in his mother's stomach.

Children of impossible odds, against an indomitable
enemy.
Who else but us would be able to carve our own
piece of heaven?
Who else but us would be allowed in a universe
where liberation is let loose?
Who else but us would be able to cut out pieces of
the promised lands
like so many have carved out our ancestors, our
possible histories, and futures untold,
whole lineages of Oba's,
whole sacred feminine traditions
found in the Rivers and the Wind,
gone.

Who else but our Indigenous distant cousins in
suffering, kinship, and shared resistance could step
up and say to the Creator: Mother, we have been
wounded by our sibling, and they have broken the
sacred trust you have given us all.

Who else but Black peoples would be the angelic
bouncers outside Thugz Mansion? Not to keep

white people out, but to laugh at white people ass as they about to learn the shocking reality: your entire cosmos, gentle and full of symphonies and notes on a page can turn on a fucking dime. I don't want to keep white people out of thug mansion, I want them at the cookout. You see, I know in incredibly rich and beautiful ways, this country can open itself up to you with stunning gestures and gifts, and I want this heavenly mansion to be like that, enticing enough that it will make you almost think it loves you. I also want those same notes on the page to turn suddenly with the ferocity that Elijah McClain experienced. I want white people to walk in and realize how wrong they were.

About everything.

Who else but Black peoples
understand how a nice day,
a nice walk,
and an open horizon can

change? Suddenly.

I pray his spirit in the Ancestral realm
is as merciful

to those who uplifted,
supported, and re-created
structures of oppression
as the officers were on the day he was
Elijah was
2Pac was
Murdered.

Or more clearly: Forgive these trespassers
as much as I forgive myself for not being there
with Elijah
Holding his tender hands.
Any neurodiverse Black person
knows Elijah's last words
by heart I mean they always come from the
heart. Why do neurotypicals think
it is just
Normal
for our children to beat each other
teachers to ignore,
and don't you dare

be poor and neurodiverse.
All I'm trying to say

in this jumble
of words
is that
I know the heart
Elijah's last word come from
the confusion at
the stark violence of the neurotypical world.

All I'm saying is
if you are neurodiverse,
autistic,
ADHD,
incorrigible,
or whatever name they come up with this week
for us,
you know those words not verbatim
or verbatim,
and through bitter experience.

This week I have
Hyperlexia Type 3
I am only "like"
the people I relate to
and still not like

the average person that I just fucking can't ...
I just can't with y'all.

I hope this sacred land allows you to enter
twerpy lil proto-fascists.
Please bring a tiki torch.
May you scream blood and soil
to much fanfare.
And may that God be merciful you encounter
there.

As merciful as the news was in its coverage.
of the murder of
well everyone.

I have begged for mercy.
Like the vision of mercy given to us by this
murdered Prince.
Son of an imprisoned and forgotten Panther Queen.

Our only reason for existence
is to complete the unbroken cycle
the Ancestors
never
got to complete.

To usher in the merciful vision

for their people
these two members of this royal house
both helped to create
so that it is as real
as the bullets flying at them
throughout time and space.

Dear Mama, don't cry,
We know you sacrificed all for us
and they stole your lovers
your heart
your babies
your revolution was so compromised by the time we
got our hands
on the scraps you saved in the same
scrapbook you would later put our middle school
pictures, flashes, scenes of the womb of the universe
I mean in your womb
Black woman of the americas.
Africa has descended
to this
place
But picture this:
your baby boy's doing good

It's actually been great since I realized
I ain't a boy
nor a man I mean where is one to find
"Manhood" that isn't just
another version of the overseer.
But your baby Queer theybie
interdimensional Messenger
has always told you that we have lived
and danced
so many times
before.
Tell the homies I'm in Heaven and they
ain't got hoods
Remind them a gilded cage
a plush coffin well appointed
rims on the side and a new contract
royalties ain't what make us
royal.
Seen a show with Marvin Gaye last night,
it had me shook
He was telling the same story
that I was telling when I was with you,
the one that set you off, about these industry cats.
Not the white ones mamma, but your own,

their disdain

Dear Divine Mama who has the title
Tilly, Afeni, Samira, and Osun,
I was drinking peppermint Schnapps, with Jackie
Wilson, and Sam Cooke
Can you imagine I mean can you picture this:
Then some lady named Billie Holiday
She sang a sweet psalm of my people
of our people I mean
our people, Mama, we are packed in this place
and we have a Psalter and a song.
I can hear it now, Mother, the song that is the
resounding word
Love it just
Sang sitting there
And as our people simultaneously
picked up their weapons,
and all the guns finally were put down
in the deep-onyx, inky-black night
on a cliff that the Angels go to weep
I sat on the edge
as the bright rosy orange of Dawn stabbed heaven's sky
kicking it with Malcolm, 'til the day came

We know why Tupac Shakur was murdered.
He represents the same thing *Fred Hampton* did.
A young charismatic leader who could
unite
the most disaffected of the
Black community,
her so-called criminals and gangs
her intellectual class and elite.
Our generals
and support staff,
our cabinet,
our congress,
our senate.
All right there for the taking.

United with an army that had already had enough.
Enough is enough. Every so-called gang in america,
particularly in the '70s rose as a response to seeing
the Panthers and others gunned down for step-
ping into the public square to defend us. Young
Black and Latino/a/x kids were sick of a generation
already seeming long in the tooth, pushing thirty
by now, telling them what to do and creating
morality around realities of the hood. They were a

response to waking to a world aflame already, and the revolution already over and lost, with most leadership being completely unaware. But if you were poor and Black in West Philly in the '70s like my dad you could at any given time be approached by the Nation of Islam, the remnants of the Panthers like Mumia Abu-Jamal and others during the advent of MOVE and John Africa's movement, or a host of other groups trying to change the city and the world through radical means. Or you could join the Moon gang. Which he did. Honestly I don't blame him. It was the only path that even had a semblance of autonomy. And fun.

That's what scared the US government about Tupac; he made the revolution look fun. When he could feel the noose tightening, death waiting to give him the best kiss of his life at his door, he even had the foresight to leave us a goodbye note from Home.

The Orun.
Heaven in colonizer.

Mumia Abu Jamal

Five

Hidden Science, from Hidden Alchemist

We all turn to the east to offer peace.
We all turn to the east to offer prayer.
So many of our traditions have us face the east from where we stand now.
Some of us not during the dawn, some of us right as the rosy amber beams
break the horizon and from the east a new day dawns.

The origin story of hip-hop
starts in the east like all good days do

in the Garden of Babylon
that is the Bronx.

When you look to the east, you expect a rising
sun, a shining star.

I expected greatness when I asked around
searched the few books, speakers, events,
and places where hip-hop was treated
like serious art.
I couldn't find
the alchemy,
primordial ingredients,
or the gumbo
that made the fertile Garden of Eden
that birthed the heart of all hip-hop.

This book is dedicated to the words, prose, field
report, and the epistemology of hip-hop.
Those who knew the unknowable.
Held the unholdable.
Those who knew the philosopher's stone was
somewhere between
the left and right side
and the crossfaaaaaaaaaadadddddddddeeeeeer.

To the DJ.
The DJ is the seer, the medium, the channeler of
vibrations, waves, and love beyond us.

Able to broadcast Ese Ifá verse of the lost tribe of
Shabaaz,
to remix the songs of the Maroons.
The very songs the Maroons had to relearn
under relearned stars
all over again to worship their Messengers
from the Divine.

Hip-hop is the library of Alexandria of the Mamas
their tears as they asked
begged, pleaded
to their Indigenous allies
fellow captives
which herbs, plants, and medicines
did the Creator use here
to keep their babies alive?
Hip-hop is the architecture of liberation
subversively drawn on blueprints
that one can only feel
(can you feel me y'all?)
in alleys, notebooks, subway walls, and hot cars.

The architect is the DJ.
Hermes Trimegas, Ptah, Orunmilla,
Progientier and Believer in the impossible destiny
of this art,
this philosophy. *My Philosophy.*

Clive.

We honor him as DJ Kool Herc.[1]

Like a lion from the gates of Zion
came this reincarnated child with the innovation
of Ogun,
the infused energy of Hallie Salisie.
This selector[2] who used electricity
with the Blessing and Charms of Shango,
who slammed sound to the ground with the clap
of Thunder
and the Applause of Oya
as she danced with Iku, death's name
to those who know how to love her
for who she is.
Perhaps it was Oya who guided Clive as he
espoused
concepts carved out the air, wind, and soundwaves

that passed the Bronx and its endless fires meant
to kill its residents.

The selector is a special interdimensional
warrior born in the deep healing energy
of the Herb. THC. Hashish.
An ancient medicine found in India (Indica),
Africa,
and eventually a major part of the healing arts of
Jamaica.
An island
nation
that had liberation in the air,
and had already sent that liberation back
to the Motherland,
the americas,
and beyond.

No one has any response to the ancient words *Jah
Rastafari*
when they land on our bodies.
From this ancient line
comes
DJ Kool Herc.
That name has the same weight.

The Break. The Merry Go Round.
Who could have known that heart of all magic for
a generation
could be born in Breaks between
James Brown's "Now clap your hands! Stomp your
feet!"
and "Bongo Rock"
by the Incredible Bongo Band. But you did.
Saint Clive of the Bronx.
You knew
a third way was possible
by the time you used the "Bongo Rock"
break to dance
us to the cold, gray, distant shores
of England and "the Mexican."

Who knew the Holy Parent of the B-Boy,
B-Girl,
B-Queer
would be the combination of NYCHA housing,
an immigrant who got the job done,
and the epistemology of the oppressed.

The Liminal Space where music reaches
to the very edges of the cosmos

to touch something
novel
trying to be born.
A Divine child infused with infinite ancestral
potentiality,
good fortune,
adventure,
enemies
and slanderers in the streets.

That is where DJ Herc helped reach into the
unknown. He helped midwife another form of the
beat and the bata, of the rhythm that helped us sing
the blues, you brought the crossroads of Mr. Johnson
to the Bronx, the Bronx to middle america.

You made a home for us. We destroyed their
charts so fast they created new ones to make it
"fair" for their artist. Armed with the Break, a
mighty tempo paradox that rocked like a flam-
ing machete headed straight for the crossroads of
Destiny and Liberation.

Two turntables and a microphone.
Music to my ears

with the power
to bring our
former masters
to their knees.

Six

One Mic and Multitudes

"All I need is one blunt, one page, and one pen
One prayer, tell God forgive me for one sin
Matter of fact, maybe more than one, look back
At all the hatred against me, fuck al of them
Jesus died at age 33, there's thirty-three shots
From twin Glocks there's sixteen apiece, that's thirty-two
Which means, one of my guns was holdin' 17
Twenty-seven hit your crew, six went into you"
                                    —Nas, "One Mic"

What would it take for a revolution?
I have sat with this question since I was seven years old

and my teacher gave us a very simplified fable
of "america"
She regaled us about knights who fought off for-
eign shackles. Brave founding fathers who planted
their pure Protestant seed into a wild and untamed
land.
And while these brave men,
only men,
made some mistakes,
some really understandable ones at that,
with those they encountered over those early
years,
we have grafted
those peoples into our glorious republic.

I can hear her sugary sweet voice say to me that
bright day in kindergarten at the end of that lovely
saga: "just like your little light, bright ass, lenny."

I swear
That's how I remember it.
Even if she didn't actually say it, my memory represents what I have taken from the ashes
of the american public education system and its
pedagogy of

oppression, systemization, identification, then
commodification.
This almost
seamless systemized radical evil
that you and I have elected to place into your,
our,
the children's minds.

What would it take to start a revolution? Even if I
buy into the fable,
at no point do I believe they intended
to ever allow us to have the tools to reshape this
republic.
For what it's worth
if you want this prize so many in this wicked land
are willing
to sell everything for:
Success.
The american dream. Wealth. McMansions and no
car note.
You can have it.

If you think that you know what's best for anyone
three hundred miles away from your community,
you are an empire.

If you're attempting to resuscitate the dream,
wipe the dust off it, and make it
"progressive,"
you are only perpetuating empire.
I don't want any part of the macabre dance
to restore the decadent palace
of the american dream to its former glory.
I am here to rob the safe.
I am here to pull out the fixtures of Washington's
bones
and teeth and hawk them.
I don't care if the former strata I couldn't reach
even exists now.
This sacred carrot held out for my descendants.
I'm not here for white man prizes anymore.

What does it take for revolution?
At the end of this long and weary day, this alt version of our country, will it take:
Thirty-three shots
From twin Glocks there's sixteen apiece, that's
thirty-two
which means, one of my guns was holdin' 17?

As a member of an endangered species
is it inevitable that one day the local body count
on the news says:
Twenty-seven hit your crew, six went into
you
Or into me
and those that I hold dear?
What does it take for a revolution?
Platform.
We have seen the best of us be platformed,
deplatformed, replatformed.

Y'all know platforms are flat right?
Only so much room on any given one?
That you can only stand there for so long before
you become
a very easy target to hit?

There is a cost for soaring,
and the cost for effectively soaring above all of
your peers for years at a time is even harder.
Nas did all this with "One Mic," where he starts
to answer the question: **What does it take for
revolution?**

It starts with one mic.
One platform.
One gallery showing.
One show.
One audition.
One dream.
One period where you had to find way more inside of you than
this country was ever willing to give you.
One time where you believe in your caramel, ebony, deep-brown, honey-colored
destiny that the Creator has crafted for you,
for Black peoples.

What does it take for a revolution? *Nas isn't telling you that.* He answers the question unknowingly. He answers the question in a way that speaks to the real-life reports of his family, friends, and his community.

Survival.
All he needed was one mic.

What will it take for a revolution? Survival.
We just need you to live beloved.

This world will testify against this empire and the stones from Queensboro will sing out …
But if platform is all you need, if my voice is enough to soften your heart, then what are eight bars to soften bullets? To soften the cuffs as they click down on my tattoos and my head is being carefully protected on its way to the plantation. My words have mentioned two Glocks, a rock from Plymouth that landed on my back and a mountaintop I'll never see, and despite the blood, sacrifice, and orations that make the heaven sing, yet this land still hasn't transformed into a country 'tis a be, nor a land of liberty.

Like Bob Marley implored us to be. Survivors. Black survivors. That's all the world had left for us.
The mic. In particular, one mic that started to create a home in my mind after *Illmatic*, suggesting that maybe I could talk about the real-life wartime conditions I grew up in with a political analysis that actually matched my lived experience. By the time "One Mic" dropped, I was ready.

For what I didn't know.

What does it take for a revolution?

The week this song dropped, April 16, 2002:
Three slain in pawnshop in Harlem
Bush 2 gave up on a two-state solution
Patriot Act 1 was bad
but it was before Patriot Act 2,
before freedom died, but after iPods.
Do you remember the fear and how we all became
Nationalist?

While Nas was dropping shit like this
and ...

revolution seemed possible. Dangerous.
It sounded like shells hitting the sidewalk for
some, and a popular consciousness shift brought
on by perhaps psychedelia for others, and whatever nascent politics Gen X slapped together after
being perhaps the most

socially engineered generation in history.

But war is a white man's prize. Peace is an illusion.
The bars of our cage are now wrapped around our
very sentience. The body keeps count, and I have
been beaten into submission.

What does it take for a revolution?
At this point, if you believe in the dream of changing this whole northern continent in some massive shift to a political structure of your design, for the many, you are thinking like a colonizer.

You don't have the right to decide
what's happening in the Bay.
Just like Oakland doesn't know what's best for our siblings in Georgia.
Imperial inclinations are just Babylonian incantations.

Dear *Brothers* who spent so much of our time at the table talking about how we could just train, arm up, organize, *and take this country*.

You want to look like those fools who burned General Washington's promise to the ground, that shred the thin ephemeral and gossamer webs that kept our barely veiled cage together in this empire?

You want to be like those on January 6, 2021, who opened the door for even their own vote not to count?

For the first time in world history, cis straight white men decided they could have a new king

without a shot fired and y'all think we are going
to do better while they rip each other to shreds?

Happened once in world history. They made sure
it would never happen again. I say again foolish
one, who do you think will be used as a shield when
they realize a two-hundred-plus-year promise
among themselves no longer can?
Our children. Our neighborhoods. Our cities that
we have kept alive since both great migrations.

What does it take for a revolution?
Absolute divergence
                from this empire,
contextual (my block) novel (new) reframing
(burned to the fucking ground)

of the concept of community,

by neighbors, neighborhoods,
neighborhood to neighborhood.

How do you *disrupt* the collective consciousness's
Passive acceptance of
murder
genocide
Queer culture being erased

hands up don't shoot
1 percent of the country having 70+ percent of the assets
the dissociative experiential state of capitalism.

How do our cities become autonomous zones, self-sustaining, through concentric circles of counter systems of mutual aid, love, need,

sacred encounter that is the midwife of
and cordially invited to
the birth of wholly separate
worlds, timelines, gardens of Eden, a second chance, new ontological realities emerging throughout what was this country?

What does it take for a revolution ???????

A perfect day.
Life. Thriving. Music. Dancing. Children with a planet that can sustain their children with full bellies.

Fire, blood, and eschaton and the archangels spearing down each other in battle is not the vision.
That's white supremacy's vision.

What does it take for revolution? *A perfect Tuesday*. Imagine: you wake up in your house. Your neighbors. Your apartment. Your world is still intact but ...

Before everything fell apart you and your neighbors pooled your money.
You bought the block and adjusted the rent of all the renters to a collectively decided amount.
You took that money, pooled it, paid, and retrofitted the utilities.

So on the day the revolution begins, that fine *Tuesday*, you hear from the local news collective fighting has broken out over the crumbs left at the table that was america. When the power goes out you're grateful everyone has solar, and you soberly listen together.

A few of the more trauma-informed care specialists in the community fan out to see how this news is impacting everyone's bodies, lives, and psyches.

You vaguely hear plans for a sacred encounter gathering tonight for those who care to join, a place to bring our Gods or none at all and let hope still grow.

As you head down to the coffeehouse that sprang up in the old police station to grab a cup, you remember how grateful you are that you and your community figured out *this* was victory.

That abolition means preparation, restoration, reparation, then liberation. By the time it all started the three square miles you and your friends had cared for and loved had been *so autonomous, for so long,* no one checked when you deployed a community safety team, with an on-staff medic, clinician, and social worker in every unit. That you had successfully ended "crime" without a shot fired. The city stopped complaining about the repairs to all the houses without a permit once you paid everyone's back taxes because money was as nascent as everything else. It was a tool that kept you from seeing each other, and once you weaponized their own system against them, they had no idea what was happening. By the time the rest of the country joined the revolution, you had already won.

One mic.
That's all we needed for one Nas.
Queensboro gets the money
and at the BBQ we pretend Uncle Nasir[1]
antivax theories ain't weird.

One mic. One thought.
One may have thought this cat faded away, but he
came with that straight-up gout,
a King's disease[2] that only those among us
who got time
not to get up and move
in this movement, has hip-hop become decadent or?

One mic. One thought. One deviation.
Is hip-hop dead?
I mean you said it Nasir, Doctor,[3]
Baron of NYC Hoodoo
I mean have you learned enough about the necro-
mancy of the capitalist machine
I mean you was the one who taught me all I
needed was

One mic. One thought. One deviation. One
Neighbor.

One neighbor I knew who loved you on Chancel-
lor Street
Kareem, that kid, man he loved you, he had a pure
heart
at the time, and ear for rhyme.
I mean

One mic. One thought. One deviation. One
Neighbor. One Neighborhood.
One neighborhood,
my neighborhood was burned down
and no one gave a fuck, would anyone give a fuck
if we just sorta took one
I mean

One mic. One thought. One deviation. One
Neighbor. One Neighborhood. One People.
What could stop that? Who could stop us?
Who has got our back? We got our back.

One mic. One thought. One deviation. One
Neighbor. One Neighborhood. One People. One
Love.
We have seen this story so many times before, so
what's it matter

If it's just God in drag, on stage,
Adorned for warfare

What does it take for a revolution?
One really good day.

When they write the story of the day we all cre-
ated our worlds
I hope they write the first line as
One day what had happened was ...

"I arrived on the same day Fred Hampton died." —Jay-Z

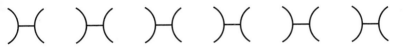

Seven

The Tragedy of St. Kanye
Jesus Walks Away

"We at war
we at war with terrorism, racism
But most of all we at war with ourselves"

—Kanye West, "Jesus Walks"

I know what you want here.
I know what he "deserves."
I don't do postmortems in front of a live studio audience
That's why I quit the church.
I can feel the bloodlust rise in some of you
as you read even this line
and slowly realize that it will not be

this story, this book, this *newer testament.*
You want me to pause in this chapter to:
rip that fucking sellout to shreds.
Psalms, scripture, music, literature, humanity is
full of stories of tragedy.
In this story
About who we are,
based off the sounds
that filled our worlds,
Kanye will be Ophelia
out on a limb, and we will divest from
the divisive war
that white supremacy has left us all in.

Kanye West is what happens to the Black artist
under the white gaze.
He has been hollowed out.
Kanye has left the building in the same way
Legion has left the building.
A perverse exorcism where we watch the white
gaze rip Kanye out
and the hordes of a hundred lies and twisting of
reality
enter his shell.

And Kanye is also like the artist that Baldwin talks about, the one who finally realizes that his suffering is insignificant, unless he uses it to connect to others' suffering. The universality of human suffering is often the artist's first breakthrough into what humanity can really offer this misfit. This Alien. This traveler from afar.

Kanye was no different.

Tired of being the one who made the molecular structure of the song, and the def jam payment plan[1] system in which producers and others find themselves relegated to poverty in the long run, Mr. West wanted to say something.

Never trust a backpack rapper with a Gucci bag.
Never trust a backpack rapper with an empty backpack.

They ain't getting on the train.
They ain't fishing in that jawn for subway tokens because the cops threw them out the park.
They ain't writing eight bars in the margins
of the margins

of the margins
of a marble composition book
while they mom clown the fuck outta they ass
at ShopRite.

Naw cats like this pull up. They PULL UP.
With a crew,
some brand-new-ass car that the payments are a
third of they hustle,
a business card,
a personal card,
QR code to his social linktr.ee,
an MP3,
a CD,
some weird neon shit in the trunk,
already got a clothing line he is showing you
while sharing it with his followers
saying shit like "we out here."
These always inviting ass people.

Inviting you to some party that is "they" party.
Gaudy flyer that says "ladies' night"
which means rock-gut,
bottom-shelf shots all night,
a champagne boat that floats by peddling
headaches,

and peers who never learned consent
in kindergarten.

These always selling ass people.

Always got some new shit they were trying to sell
you on,
because their old shit was knowledge,
wisdom, and understanding
and was in fact, *true indeed,*
but new science dropped on 'em.
So MAGA. Or whatever the fuck.

These beautiful Black people
who look into the abyss of this country
and when it looks back: *like what they see.*

They imagine they have a kinship with the dragon
they have just discovered,
the ability to use words, images, metaphors,
language and it's deconstruction
and reconstruction in the grand art of
moving the juggernaut of the human psyche
forward,
or backward,
or in your pocket,

or in your ear,
or you could also put it in your heart and take the
martyr's path.

I imagine a young Kanye to be everything we meet
in a College Dropout. That, and much afterward,
was real.
As real and visceral as a noose around one's neck,
as the knife placed to one's throat by an enemy,
as real as
the collision of stars that happened hundreds of
millions of years ago
that we are just seeing the lights from today.

The eyes of the abyss,
Tartarus,
inferno,
the emptiness, the great rending of tomorrow,
that is the white gaze in this country.
When the white gaze starts to affix itself on you,
you don't recognize it.

But it recognizes you.

And that shit feels great. I remember when I realized it was turning its coal-red eyes upon me,

this great beast, this towering scarlet Babylon,
with its wings and long jaw.
You don't know the white gaze is white.
It feels like the world is looking at you
and that's the lie.

In this country, where so many of us are invisible,
when you are finally allowed to
see the inner workings, shoestrings, bubblegum,
and hope that holds together
the grand mechanism that is capitalism,
When you become cursed with the hex:
Celebrity,
vexing and frustrating
personal wealth poisoning our dreams.
We have been taught
that to be in the gaze of the great serpent of old
is a victory,
as an artist all you want to do is provoke it.
Tempt it to destroy you.
Mock it. Make fun of it.
Warn others about what is
and what is not this country.
It's people.

Our story.

And as it first starts moving toward you, this dragon, you are either foolish enough to believe you can defeat it or already in love with the reflection of yourself you can see in its eyes.

The white gaze. It looks at you when you notice it.

we at war

we at war with terrorism, racism

But most of all we at war with ourselves

And it warps you.

Burns you to the ground. It took an artist who had people saying the name of Jesus Nazareth in the club at 2:00 a.m. and made him dance the jig for white supremacy, by weaponizing a hidden mental illness crisis in the same social media culture that propelled him to fame. Death by medium.

For the Black artists, if their own creations don't eat them, or they don't go mad, then the white gaze will eat them alive.

And don't try to escape: Just ask Mother Lauryn.

But the truth is one cannot abandon the road the timeline, the earth, the country, and

white supremacy and still exist.
I mean if you are reading this
it's in the water.
Of course as Uncle Jimmy
Sage Baldwin
the Gay nigga you ignore
the poet
he prophesied over us
"The Artist"

"And yet people, millions of people whom you will
never see, who don't know you, never will know
you, people who may try to kill you in the morning, live in a darkness which—if you have that
funny terrible thing which every artist can recognize and no artist can define—you are responsible
to those people to lighten, and it does not matter
what happens to you."[2]

You think it matters to you
what happens to Kanye
me, Biggie, Jam Master J?
There is a 51 percent chance of
death by

bullet
if you're a modern-day poet.
Do the math
these cats did.[3]

The white gaze, this book, my life
the life of a Black artist
in this land it is useful.

For as God in drag as a man said as the Avatar
Baldwin:

"You are being used in the way a crab is useful,
the way sand certainly has some function. It is
impersonal."[4]

If you saying how can they be back on this talk,
there I said it.

Just like Jimmy said:

"This force which you didn't ask for, and this
destiny which you must accept, is also your
responsibility. And if you survive it, if you don't
cheat, if you don't lie, it is not only, you know,
your glory, your achievement, it is almost our

only hope—because only an artist can tell, and only artists have told since we have heard of man, what it is like for anyone who gets to this planet to survive it."[5]

Kanye went to the
Pearly Gates and fell.
We recorded it.

White men do this every day in silence.

Y'all mad because Kanye didn't
survive america? The white gaze.
Jury still out on you fam.
You could also
just
get out.

"After all, there is a kind of saving egotism too, a cruel and dangerous but also saving egotism, about the artist's condition, which is this: I know that if I survive it, when the tears have stopped flowing or when the blood has dried, when the storm has settled, I do have a typewriter which is my torment but is also my work. If I can survive it, I can

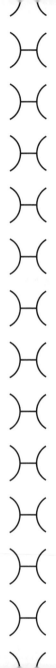

always go back there, and if I've not turned into a total liar, then I can use it and prepare myself in this way for the next inevitable and possibly fatal disaster. But if I find that hard to do—and I have a weapon which most people don't have—then one must understand how hard it is for almost anybody else to do it at all."[6]

Maybe Kanye ain't the only one who is
Fucked.
Just get out.

Eight

Mother Lauryn

"Oh, you'd be smart to save your soul
Oh, when escape is mind control
You spent your life in sacrifice
To a system for the dead
Oh, are you sure ...
Where is the passion in this living
Are you sure it's God you servin'
Obligated to a system
Getting less then you're deserving
Who made up these schools, I say
Who made up these rules, I say
Animal conditioning
Oh, just to keep us as a slave
Oh, just get out"

—Lauryn Hill, "I Get Out"

Get out.
Get out of your box. Your system. Your cage.
Gilded with all the accouterments of near
freedom.
america is a holding cell
and you are a lifer
waiting to be assigned to the next facility.
Like any part of the prison-industrial complex
it is designed
to move
right
past the average oblivious citizen
like an undertow
whose pull can only be felt by a few.
The way that it all seamlessly fits together
to create the
illusion
of safety.
Constructs of civility,
polite society,
and a people determined to make the world
into a progressive
utopia

even if they have to wipe us all out on the
way.

Get out.
Get out of the snake pit
you are using as a life raft
to get through the never-ending
hurricane that is capitalism.
Get out of the heteronormative 4.5-member
household
that seems to be perfectly adjusted
for inflation, COLA rate,
and the latest market forecast.
Get out of your fucking clothes already
with someone you love.
Get out of the illusion
you and your ancestors
have been here four hundred years,
their crime started then,
the pool of blood spreads from there.

But if you are Black in the northern americas you
have a 70+ percent
chance of being descended from kingdoms

that weren't discovered until 1830s.
That had been lost to whiteness since *Nero*.
That thirty years after being discovered the way a
Black writer is
by publishers,
meaning
they profitable
and thousands of miles away,
these same ancestors would rise up en masse
and take up arms against half their captors and
have a taste of what this land calls "freedom."

Get out of the idea the world has always been like this.
It's a trap.
Its empiricism.
It's death.
It's the enlightened crystallization of reality.

Get out of eschaton.
Get out of the end.
Get off the cliff's edge,
and stop believing that Babylon wants to see any
of us fly.

Rage and get out.
Get out of the neocolonial last-ditch effort
to fight over dinosaur bones
and lifeless barren rocks
hundreds of thousands of years older than
democracy.

Mother Lauryn was born in the fallen lands of the
Bricks.
Sister Lauryn was from another land.
Lauryn's voice cut through the bricks
of every apartment in Philly
the summer my daughter was preparing to enter
this world,
this marketplace,
this prison,
this cage.

I was in a cage by that fall.
While the miseducation of Lauryn was made
apparent to all,
my education was just about to start being born
in Black male body.

It was in Montgomery county prison
(their term and title)
when this string of impossible words became my
joy, my Zion.

I was laying on the top bunk
staring
at the soft fluorescent light
that never quite went off at night,
as the dawn approached.
The guard jangled his keys
and yelled out a series of commands, phrases,
and other things every few hours
to disrupt our rest in the singsong voice
and baritone of a Black man quite happy
to cage up everybody in the neighborhood
who don't act right.
As he stomped past in his chains
that he most likely was never able to see,
he slid a letter under the door of my two-man pod
like cell for kitchen workers,
and with that woosh of paper
on institutional waxed floor
I was introduced to the rest of my life.

Lauryn stepped into her power post Fugees,
then offered the explanation why she left
as the soundtrack of the summer
we were all having in Black america.
The summer of 1998 I was ragged
from the West Coast
and trapped in the concrete jungle of the East Coast.
Sitting in the dilapidated throne my line planted
in what was left for us
in the empire.
That was Sixty-Second and Race Street.
Again.

August 25, 1998/Miseducation of
Lauryn Hill
Dddddddddddddddddrrrrrrrroooppppppppppppped
I mean you can feel the beat?
And before you
GOT OUT
On May 7, 2002,
"Terrorist Missile Strikes" entered the lexicon.
A new gift to the Sudan I mean we had already
forgotten
the Serbs hunting Albanians.

Sheesh look at me getting all
misty-eyed for the Clinton
regime and war criminals.

I mean what was their main focus that year ...?
Ohhh yeah ruining a fucking young woman's life.
Monica becomes Jezebel.
Clinton balanced the budget so you animals

murdered Matthew Shepard.
If it is ever to be one world family,
then I apply to adopt the spirit
of Matthew Shepard.
That's just 1998.

MK Ultra's[1] product
organic weapon, no the other one,
not Leary, not Kesey, not the nice boomer white
dad who didn't go full fascist
Thanks, Bob.

No the other totally cool experiment from the
'60s psychedelic
era of exploration where the pure of the midwest
tasted the divine.
The other totally safe experiment from those
times,

Terry Nichols.
The Unabomber met his fate.
1998 ended with you leaving hip-hop
and the results of the Technicolor psychedelic
war of the '60s.
The drug war was about more than your hustle,
homie
We got Terry Nichols, cuz.

Whiteness's last attempt
to understand
Indigenous science, "plant medicine" on insta.

Colonizers on the astral plane fam.
Astral plane ain't even
the name.
First they take the words.
Orwell was some Black woman.
Take 'em back.

And by the time you said:
Get. Out.
May 7, 2002

PALESTINE FOREVER
Even though Bush decided two states

was not as good as one
colonizer state.
If you think Yasser Arafat
was the problem, you should go hang
with your friendly
Texas evangelical homie.

Bernard Law: defrocked in the eyes
of they stolen God
and Boston "Law" comes for
The throne of St. Peter.

Corruption finally speeds into our community in a
frightening way.
In the same way we refuse to own Kanye
we won't own:
John Allen Muhammad and John Lee Malvo.
I mean if Blackness ain't a monolith
they can stand alone
and still be
of us.

But if I could go back to
those hazy midsummer days
of
August 25, 1998,

when *Miseducation*
dropped,

I would use these words as the Orikki
Invocation.
May these evocative words be an
evocation to beg her to
get out:

Dear america, may my daughter have a bit of your
bread and cup?
May she too be poisoned by its bitter taste?
May her stomach become full of the bile
and rot that wretches back up
at you in defiant displays of life and art.

May she use the ashes
of what I was
to start a fire
in her own life that unravels
who she is
in this place.
this cage.

Dear daughter,
Mother

Lauryn wore a crown,
they are heavy,
they slip off,
they are often carried inelegantly
and hard to balance
because of the
killing gaze
of the constructs of whiteness.

Dear daughter, she was born in the Bricks,
and although your mom dragged you off to Mainline
to be born,
you were baptized,
like every Duncan before you,
in the struggle for joy
in the same bedroom
as my brother and I.

You walked up to Marrones
and grabbed a water ice
with coins stuffed in your stroller
like every child/omo of our line before you I know of.

Three generations slowly strolling
up the same half block

through space time
and you may not remember
that brief time
with us, but the ancestors do.

Olodumare does.

You are a witness.
Like every witness before you in our line.
What you can perceive may help others see.
You drank of that deep feeling of those days
walking Race Street
just like any of these three generations
I know and love.
I stand on Sixty-Third and Race
looking toward the El May 13, 1985,
watching smoke rise.
I stand on the corner in fall '99,
or maybe it's the fall of 2K ...

I stand on Sixty-Third and Race
waiting to cross the street
to go get a water ice with you,
daughter. Mother
Lauryn is still wafting past even

though they digitally lynched her
with one of the most all-encompassing
media smear
campaigns by one DJ
who had a show to sell.
And why not sell it on the naive,
wondrous,
number one
back
of a piece of art birthed by a Black Messenger
from better worlds and better days.
Ciphers complete, cycles,
wheels lurch into place and for a second

Dear Daughter, dear ancestors
I can see where we both stand
along the tracks our bloodline
laid out for us.

Amen. Ase. Jenna, Make your life be.

For *all* its well documented
and "critiqued" flaws,
Miseducation
is an

education
in what one lone siren of the deep rivers of
Western Africa,
of the Hudson,
of the Schuylkill,
of the Delaware,
of forgotten steel lakes awash in the rust of an
industrialized world
that found cheaper victims,
what a sorceress
of the living Logos,
the Word,
the very pattern of the Creator,
can drag into this wicked world
with enough will.

Lauryn shined, even when her own light seemed
to go out.

Dear daughters of the diaspora
I am not fit
To untie the thong of your
Sandals.
Dear weary ass messiahs,

when I was
Mother Lauryn's age
when she wrote this honey-dipped scroll of
prophecy
I couldn't even articulate my first thought as an
artist.

Dear daughters of Assata,
I stand on the corner of Sixty-Third and Race
still peering toward impossible futures
full of anticapitalist constructs,
free peoples having access to the project of
discovering
human liberty.
I see you.
I love you.
Before you believe them remember
we were warned:

Oh, you'd be smart to save your soul
Oh, when escape is mind control
You spent your life in sacrifice
To a system for the dead
Oh, are you sure ...

Where is the passion in this living
Are you sure it's God you servin'
Obligated to a system
Getting less then you're deserving
Who made up these schools, I say.
Who made up these rules, I say.
Animal conditioning
Oh, just to keep us as a slave
Oh, just get out
Of this social purgatory.
Just get out
All these traditions are alive
Just get out

Trayvon Martin

Nine

I See No Changes, Just COINTELPRO

"Come on, come on

I see no changes, wake up in the morning, and I ask myself

Is life worth living, should I blast myself?

I'm tired of bein' poor, and even worse I'm Black

My stomach hurts, so I'm lookin' for a purse to snatch

Cops give a damn about a negro

Pull the trigger, kill a nigga, he's a hero

Give the crack to the kids who the hell cares

One less hungry mouth on the welfare

First, ship 'em dope and let 'em deal the brothers

Give 'em guns, step back, watch 'em kill each
other
It's time to fight back, that's what Huey said
Two shots in the dark, now Huey's dead"

—2Pac, "Changes"

I write this particular part of our psalm in the fall
of '23.

I see no changes.
All I see is changed allies. Accomplices. Anarchists.
Switched up.
Lost steam.
Gave up because ...

It's been
2 years
24 months
96 weeks
730 days
17,520 hours
1,051,200 minutes
63,072,000 seconds
Since May 25, 2020.

At the moment of typing, writing, ranting, creating, dying, being reborn.

The first time someone told me about the conspiracy against the Black man,
I stood wide-eyed
and light-skinned AF
mostly chewing licorice root
happy to be included.
I loved to hang with these cats who called me half unoriginal
man.
It's not that I disagreed with their conclusions.
I agreed.
Half man half amazing.
Half masculine half angelic.
For sure
something queer
here.
But almost immediately I saw that the most important pieces were missing from the picture they were painting, these cats with so many uncited, ill-researched, poorly informed, but well fucking meaning:

"facts"
that constructed the arguments which, while believable,
at times, left a lot on the table.

It left Black: Queers
   Woman
   Free Expression
   Art
   Innovation
   Spirituality
   Unless it was all shaped a particular way.

Heteronormativity.
You know the shape
You know what it is

All I see is changes.
I see no changes.
Nothing has changed from the moment I heard Kurt Lowder announce the panther prince's murder in my hotel room, God knows where, after another night trying to Psychonaut out of white

supremacy.

I got the report right as I was reentering the
Earth's atmosphere.
I did not see this Shakur leave us,
I was quite sure I could hear in the distance
another who wept.
Like Nas said
I swear in that moment
I dreamed of
Afeni Shakur.
'cause like Loretta Duncan
'cause like Ann Jones,
she raised a ghetto king.
In my case I accept the title
Sovereign of the Streets
in a war.

How do you prove fifty years of social engineering?
How do you prove that the police, the media, and the
protectors of the "homeland" have spent a century
trying to keep your family line in place. In check. In
one area. Inside the prison-industrial complex.

Me and my father were never very close in life;
this is why I am grateful for ancestral practices,

altars, and those of us who know we are products of hundreds of moves, decisions, sacrifices, and resistance from hundreds of generations before us.

Me and my father were never close in life, but ten years after *Loving v. Virginia*, he tried to raise me in the burbs.
Doylestown PA.
Two plants. Three inches high. Planted in a small terrarium in the living room as entertainment.
The charge was manufacturing.
I wasn't close to my father: because in these critical years when
I should have been in his arms, he was in prison.
One or two plants, most likely both male and unable to make
buds. I wish me and my dad were better buds.

I wasn't given a chance to see
no changes.
All I ever saw was:

COINTELPRO, or in full Counterintelligence Program, is a program conducted by the FBI from 1956 to 1971 to discredit and neutralize organizations considered subversive to US political stability. It was covert and often used extralegal means to criminalize various forms of political struggle and derail several social movements, such as those for civil rights and Puerto Rican independence.

COINTELPRO operations were initiated against various organizations, including the Communist Party, Socialist Workers Party (SWP), Puerto Rican Nationalist Party, Black Panther Party (BPP), American Indian Movement, Southern Christian Leadership Conference, and Ku Klux Klan. Tactics included intense surveillance, organizational infiltration, anonymous mailings, and police harassment. These programs were exposed in 1971 when the Citizens' Commission to Investigate the FBI burglarized an FBI office in Media, Pennsylvania, stole confidential files, and then released them to the press. More information regarding COINTELPRO was later obtained through the Freedom of Information Act, lawsuits lodged against the FBI by the BPP and the SWP, and statements by agents who came forward to confess their counterintelligence activities.[1]

All I ever saw was in big block letters, crime in the city.
All I ever saw was that I was a weapon, or I could be weaponized.
All I ever saw was change: in body count
in the shape of my cage
in the structures of oppression sold as the next hand up.

All I ever saw change was the art.

Scat and do wap
has become bop bop bop bop bop.
The sound of the merry-go-round and the break
and shells dropping to the ground.
Cowries would be preferable
to the bullet casings.
The sound of shells and
bop bop bop bop bop bop.
It seemed while we had 2Pac,
america was about to get theirs.

In the hands of 2Pac Shakur
the dynamite
that was Black youth power
that made J. Edgar Hoover's Jowl,
quiver in the night.
A Black messiah made of lyrical
C4 gel packs stuck to
every white kid in the suburban
mind
eating away their apathy
making poor J. Edgar's
jowls flap
like wings in the night of the nether realm.

Don't believe me: go to
https://vault.fbi.gov/cointel-pro

Go right there on the FBI website.
Go see the crimson pools of blood intermingle
with the indigo and white of this flag, this promise,
this vision, this dream,
this panther prince was cut down.
This panther prince was
complicated.

This panther prince most likely was never taught
about consent, or the value of using our bodies like
holy vessels for the Orisha
to meet,
to dance,
to make love.

Or maybe he was.
I am not here to wipe away anything.
I'm here to uncover, or get uncovered
But I know not knowing
that stuff can put a young star,
and those in his orbit in danger.

This monstrous scene we call the policing of
american thought.
Black thought.
The FBI, the average cat on the street, the solid
revolutionary, they all thought they would see
changes.
I see no changes.
I only see the armed enforcers of capitalism
I only see a lot of us being removed from the
board. Just enough that the next generation

doesn't know the rules. Or that our lives are a game to them.

Cops give a damn about a negro
Pull the trigger, kill a nigga, he's a hero

Well, now this hero is running for senate. He is campaigning on my death.
He is on Pennsylvania Avenue because he is willing to pull the trigger, kill a nigga, he's a hero.
He is the president of the united states.

Our adversary in this land will become
a lot of things.
Perhaps a cop, perhaps my new boss, perhaps an armed stranger who has decided
today is the day someone pays
for the existence of Blackness.
And like a shadow given legs to walk,
It strolls down the road
and shifts
from the forty-fifth presidential manifestation of evil
at the ohhh sooo fucking white house.

Who is this adversary?
Old Scratch. Shaitan. The archangel that is the
most like unto God.
The Leviathan. The slanderer in the street. The
malignancy.
The devil.
Fact or fiction,
creation of God or human,
it doesn't make his power
any less.
I call him by his proper name in this age:
white supremacy.
"He" is exactly why we need the panther prince.

Hip-hop,
its prophets,
its messages,
and even its hopes of being an art
in a hundred years
is broken,
flawed,
and wrong at times.
So incredibly wrong.
Perhaps hip-hop is
the rawness of lines

that feel like a wisdom
from the Creator
come to help you in
overstanding[2] america.
Lines that put words
to an experience
you
have been having
your
whole life
in one moment.

Yet give you deep secondhand embarrassment
that you ever
shouted to your boy
yelled to your girl at the club
repeated to your partner like Holy Scripture,
or wrote on your spiral notebook
that same line
five years later.

The brassiness of an art form
that is willing to be wrong.

"He" will never stop coming until he has his
property back. Us.

If Malcolm was our manhood
stolen
then this was the revenge attack on his little
brother
during the funeral.
Only in america
can you be born on a battlefield
and then be blamed for going to war.
Only in america can they hand you bullets
instead of crayons and
you become a deadly weapon.
Only in america
the most populous people in the world
at one point can become an endangered species.

For all the things that can only happen in america
I am grateful 2Pac is one of them.

Ten

Manufactured in america

"Sweet King Martin, sweet Queen Coretta
Sweet Brother Malcolm, sweet Queen Betty.
Sweet Mother Mary, sweet Father Joseph
Sweet Jesus, we made it in America
Sweet baby Jesus, oh sweet baby Jesus ..."

—Jay-Z and Kanye West, "Made in America"

I am a product of the united states of america.

So was the song "Made in America." It dropped in 2011. That's all the context Jay and Kanye give us, and arguably, this is the height of what I would call the second wave of hip-hop. That's how powerful these dudes were. The walking tragedy that Kanye

was already showing signs of being, and america's favorite hustler out of the projects, Jay-Z.

They are so enthroned in the white gaze's power that they named the album *Magna Carta*, and at one point on the album, if you listen closely, Jay lays out the basic arguments of Socrates, Aristotle, and other philosophers just to show he can.[1]

Hip-hop even had its own aging stars doing revival tours, church groups that taught "hip-hop" dance. I mean we got introduced to Hamilton by Obama's attempt to normalize hip-hop in the white house and guess who was invited?
Lin.

Look this song for me is like if you could go back to the moment
the levees broke during Katrina, or see
the moment the Tower of Babel slowly rocked back and forth, or
when African leaders
in the early eighteenth century realized
how fucked they were.
That's this moment in hip-hop.

The poetry that follows is my attempt
to understand the Tower card from the Tarot.
To understand the Leviathan. To understand a
mass shooter seconds before they strike. This is
the madness that infects us all.
It makes me wonder why evil things happen to
good art.

Manufactured in america:

Like a geode split open,
a vein of gold discovered in between territories,
like rare earth metals that our corporate masters

will send our young folks off to die for soon,
I was formed in unique elements
that combined under almost incomprehensible
amounts of time and pressure.

I am a product of the united states of america.
Nowhere else
a decade after *Loving v. Virginia*

could my daddy romance
my mamma on their first
free weekend
from a rehabilitation program

in Quakertown founded
possibly by Rosicrucians.
Only in america
could I have asked a then scrappy

presidential candidate
William Jefferson Clinton
a question
so precocious

I made ABC news
as a gangly almost teen hotep.

My first national news story
for being Black
and inquisitive
about this Babylon system.
It wouldn't be my last.

I was designed this way.
I was manufactured
to fail
just like my
youthful rebellion.
Just like my revolution
and its vision
I had firmly planted in my heart.

Just like everything
I ever come in contact
with in this land.

Architecture designed
to let "exceptional"
Black persons ride the winds
of what Babylon calls ire,[2] good fortune.
The path is just high enough
so they can see the limits of the prison they are in.
Just above the flotsam, waste, and other floating
bodies of your siblings.

As the tides of capitalism slowly drag their bloated,
twisted forms out to a sea
to make room
for the next batch of fools
who listened to the siren song
that is success
in this land.

I have a barcode they put under my toe,
just in case I "make it."

I made it in america.
It would be hard for me to deny the fact

that there hasn't been a ceiling
I haven't
touched
in this country.
I don't know how
watching a blackbird
trapped, flailing
for open skies,
squawking,
lost in a building
they never asked to be housed in,
Rehoused
Relocated in.
A dream
they never fell asleep for,
This parody we call Black Success
Is it a success?
It doesn't feel like success, it feels like
a hallway full of mirrors and all the reflections are
the enemy.
Or rather in america success is a reflection of the
enemy
that looks like you, your dreams, your happiness.

But who put these strange thoughts in your head
for land that
ISN'T YOURS?
Hunks of metal to take you afar
to shop
work
floss
shine
STUNT ON THESE NIGGAS
in the reason your grandchildren won't be able to
breathe
the air outside.
Put 20s on that shit.

But it is.

In america
the fact
that I was allowed to fly high
enough
to hit the ceiling is proof
to half the country
that the ceiling does not exist.
To make it in america

is to stick your plumage out
for white america
to inspect,
and decide
if it is decadent enough
to be marveled at
and safe enough
to be absorbed by its children.

They cut Malcolm X down
because he was our Shango.
They let Kanye sing
because they knew they would be writing his
songs.
They hunted King Martin
until the fear
was just another layer
the assassin's bullet
had to cut through.
They watched Jay-Z make it in america
with perhaps the most bemused joy of all,
excited one of the hustler nation
would become a billionaire
and would bring the pathogen

back to us.
Who wants to rub elbows with that?
Capitalism is our smallpox-infested blankets
and clothing.
A gift
from your friends
down the road

Best to send gifts back to the Black children of
the americas.

The trap in america
is that you can make it.
The trap is that you fucking make it. You are in the
trap now.
The trap is the hustle
That trap is you can make it.
That you *do make it.*
That you do get an agent.
You do get invited
out to speak,
teach,
share ciphers of knowledge, wisdom, and under
standing,

and that's because
white america
has heard it all before.
You think you are
Something new?
I
I thought ...

You thought motherfucker.

I thought
because I found the path,
and the machete someone left behind,
that I was a trailblazer,
not a participant in colonization.

Capitalism is a blanket full of smallpox, and I came
home bearing gifts.

Coretta was left to hold babies,
shattered stained-glass pieces of the steeple
movement
of Black Liberation
with a few Queers in the back doing the grunt
work.

Who suits the cause of those who

wore suits of Armor made of
respectability,
and prophetic power
that was taken in a second,
in a muzzle flash,
in a bright
pop
of humanity
being cut down.

Romana Africa wasn't given a chance to hold the
babies,
the Philly Police Department decided
it was tidier
to let
the
fire
burn.
Queen Betty, what are we to do with your sorrow,
dedication, and love?
Kadijah[3] reborn.
Where are we to lay

the Prophet Malcolm's (PBUH)[4]
body?

Assata just sucks in her breath
from a market in Cuba,
another hot
day
in exile.
The only way to be made in america
is to be
made in america™
thus you aren't surprised when
you are destroyed
by america.

Perhaps they just want us to keep up
the Black labor of
making america.
After all she hungers still for:
Martyrs.
Prophets.
Artists.
Revenue.
Prison Population.
Boogeymen.

Queens Who Birth Monsters.
Court Jesters.
Heroes Turned Inside Out.
Women behind Bars, Midwifing Capital.
Black Bodies.

SWEET JESUS!!!!!
WE MADE IT
IN AMERICA
WE ARE MADE
IN AMERICA
SWEET BABY JESUS
WE ARE IN
america.

When this song dropped it
used to bring tears to my eyes.
It truly felt
like a new Black america's
anthem.
It felt like a dope festival
in my hometown
of 215
jungles.

It felt like the resurrection of our deities
after an attempted deicide.

Written in the crimson
blood pools of the flag
of this country,
but elders now in the skin of their children, living,
bright, and golden teachers from the ancestral
realm.

Knew that shit was too good to be true.

In the year of the white MAGA lord 2022
on a brisk fall day
before I head out into the Sun
I can see the shadows across everyone
in this story,
I can see america trying
to
swallow us.

From overt support of perhaps
an orange slab of meat
animated by the nether realms
if not *the,*
then *one* of European Christianity's

vaunted "antichrists."
With more sure to come.
What else could american evangelicalism produce
other than Donald Trump?
Name another fruit that could grow
from that vine?
What else but the music industry
could produce Kanye West?
What other vine
but this one
with its particular brand of
Black intellectual and
artistic exploitation,
destruction,
literally
pressing the rind of our bodies
to squeeze another
dollar out of us before tossing us
into the wastebasket of modernity,
could this parody of their own self grow
from anywhere else but this bitter vine?

Let's contemplate demons
creatures that take a kid
from Marcy with

reasonable doubt,
or maybe he just picked 12,[5]
or maybe it was all smoke
and mirrors
and just one long-ass
crypto scam.
After all, I mean
after all this,
it's just all white man prizes,
and it never feels like
victory at all.

"Sweet King Martin, sweet Queen Coretta
Sweet Brother Malcolm, sweet Queen Betty,
Sweet Mother Mary, sweet Father Joseph
Sweet Jesus, we made it in America
Sweet baby Jesus, oh sweet baby Jesus ..."

You can't save us from ourselves.
You couldn't save yourselves.
We should just try to save each other.

Sweet Jesus, we made it in america
Sweet baby Jesus, oh sweet baby Jesus ...

Eleven

My Granma Don Tol' Me, My Grandad Don Tol' Me, My Umi . . .

"I don't wanna write this down
I wanna tell you how I feel right now
Don't wanna take no time to write this down
I wanna tell you how I feel right now, hey
Tomorrow may never come
For you or me
Life is not promised
Tomorrow may never show up
For you and me
This life is not promised"

—Mos Def and Yasiin Bey, "The Mighty"

I don't want to write this down, this defense, this treatise, this love note passed to my older self from the sweaty palms of my middle school self.

Do you still love the five pillars of hip-hop? Circle yes

or no?
This whole book is
me hesitantly circling
yes.
Yes to the homophobia, and weird ass vaccine theories,
hoteps[1]
So many hoteps.
What a fucking dumb idea.
Like I need more attacks
based on my personhood and my very right to write
or speak
or be in the spaces and
body I was born with.

The hoteps will be armed
with they well-honed

but oooooohhhsooooo
true indeed
critical
miscegenation theory
bullshit,
yes to the sexual violence
aimed at the Divine Feminine,
yes to fruits
of capitalism.

I refuse to make the same move
as popular religious
and theological thinkers
running from intellectual fire
to intellectual fire
from critical analysis to critical analysis
that may lead to collective cognitive
                    leaps for Black peoples

as a people group,
but take a short
cut
that leads me to lionizing,
defending,

and or cornered
with the worst parts
of myself.
Mirror reflections
in a carnival hall of mirrors
and my now former aeons lived long ago,
or is it lives
lived long ago.

Maybe it's like the Kybalion says:

"And Death is not real, even in the Relative sense—it is but Birth to a new life—and You shall go on, and on, and on, to higher and still higher planes of life, for aeons upon aeons of time. The Universe is your home, and you shall explore its farthest recesses before the end of Time. You are dwelling in the Infinite Mind of THE ALL, and your possibilities and opportunities are infinite, both in time and Space. And at the end of the Grand Cycle of Aeons, when THE ALL shall draw back into itself all of its creations—you will go gladly, for you will then be able to know the Whole Truth of being At One with THE ALL. Such is the report of the Illumined—those who have advanced well along The Path."[2]

Prophets, heroes, seers, and other creators of
words, beats, time signatures, 88s, and moogs,
spend days sitting alone in a dark room with the
creature
the monster
the guardian angel
the devil in the mirror
that won't leave you alone, won't let you live,
won't let you breathe until you face this adversary,
this savior
this muse
this baying voice who won't shut the fuck up in
your ear.
Your Art. Your thing

that makes you special, that plucked your dumb
ass from your mama's house,
your grannie's house,
your dad's crib,
and put you   out here.

Baldwin says:

"And this is where the whole question in
my own private, personal case of being an

American artist, of being not yet sixty-
five years old, and of being an American
Negro artist in 1963 in this most peculiar
of countries begins to be a very frightening assignment."[3]

Umi said to shine my light on the world:
But what if she was wrong?
What if she was so fascinated
that we have so much inherent beauty
in me
in you
she never once factored into her equation that
america
wouldn't see the same thing.
While she saw a young Ogun sparks and engineering,
america
saw another buck to break.
Where she saw Osun dancing across the waters in
all her shades,
america
saw another piece of property.

Umi, what if you were wrong?
What if this world

Doesn't deserve
our light?
What if it's not up to the light to decide
when it shines
but us?
What if our egos are the only thing
in the way keeping it
from shining bright?

Umi what if it was all
just a ploy to show our wings,
to take flight like the Aluko bird[4]
in Western African shores,
and as soon as they spot our bright colors,
our plumage ...

Is there a bullet in the back of our heads?

Ohhhh Umi I am not afraid of the light,
but what it will reveal
about the world once I
shine it.
When the mighty Mos Def dropped
Black on Both Sides
The orange ghoul thought he would
run for president for the first time.

October of '99
I can't help but think
if we hadn't clowned him so hard ...

Fall of '99 we was so innocent.
You think back,
before terror become an enemy.
How does one defeat fear?

This is before we learned it was by breaking people.
I had heard mighty Mos Def
but October '99
I could hear Mos.

Umi says
was a reminder,
another turn of the wheel
of Black art.
It had gravity of its own,
caused whole constellations of artists
to realign.
"Umi says"

You are nothing more
than a product

of your ancestors.
If you resist,
it's because *resistance* is in your blood.
If you create art,
it's because *art* is in your bones.
If you are an abolitionist,
it's because *liberation*
is in your marrow.
If you see the brokenness in this land,
it's because of *love*.
Love is in your eyes now.
You can't unsee the pain
all around you in this country,
this city, this neighborhood,
this block you read this on now.

*Umi, I can't unsee it; Umi, I can't unsee it; Umi, I
can't unsee it.*

I shined my light and
I saw it all.
I shined my light
and it all saw me.
It looked back

at me, Umi.

When mighty Mos Def dropped, Umi says,
it was before
he was Yasiin Bey
and before Guantanamo Bay
became part of the lexicon,
a threat,
a home
for the ummah[5],
and a coffin for freedom in the twenty-first
century.

We are now dripped in words like Abu Ghraib,
Instead of singing Allahu Akbar's
and picking up dates in hot cars,
and I have to wonder
that if there is no covenant,
no great new deal,
I mean in america it's:
no deals
no forty acres,
no mule,
no respect
for Washington's promise

of a peaceful transition
no shot of
Lincoln's invitation back into humanity
being fulfilled.
What I mean by this I can still, I can still feel it
The shot in the back of Lincoln's head.

If Mos is right and "Life is not promised"
are we even alive now?
"Tomorrow may never show up,"
but most things worth dying for
I'll never see.
It's a gift for our children
"for you and me"
this is all we got,
we have a responsibility
to shine a light in the darkness.

Umi
they asked for my poetry
I gave them a sword.
I cut them to the core
and they liked it.
Swarming me as I write this to lap up their own
lifeblood

in an attempt to spill my blood.
Life is mostly blood.
Blood is mostly art.
My art is a knife.
If you cut yourself
and freeze your blood on a knife
in the winter
and wait
wolves will lick the edge.

You either got something enticing, fragrant,
in your blood,
or you don't.
You can't put it in your blood if it ain't there ...
Umi Gert, Umi Helen, Umi says ...

SHINE YOUR MUTHAFUCKING LIGHT ON
THIS SAD TRIFLING ASS WORLD

Watch the rats run.

Twelve

It Was All a Dream

"Yeah, this album is dedicated
To all the teachers that told me I'd never amount to
nothin'
To all the people that lived above the buildings that I was
hustlin' in front of
Called the police on me
When I was just tryin' to make some money to feed
my daughter (It's all good)
And all the niggas in the struggle
You know what I'm sayin'? It's all good, baby baby
It was all a dream, I used to read Word Up! Magazine"

—The Notorious B.I.G., "Juicy"

This book is dedicated to:
every class traitor
cop
judge
probation officer
counselor
ex-friend.

All y'all who said: you ain't never going to be shit.
You going to die just like your father.
That I was a fraud.
That there was nothing special about me.

To the people
who told me in my early church organizing days
when we thought we would change

everything, to stop.
Those who treated us like a bunch of kids playing
in a sandbox.

Yes, you: this book is a *real flex* on
you
traitor to the movement.

You have hidden in pews, seminaries, pulpits,
theology,
social media activist for Jesus who is

sooo progressive the average Black person ain't
good enough.
Who the fuck is you helping?

The progressive mainline church
so intersectional
many of its Uncle Toms
and Juans
told me straight the fuck up:
that we were *not*
an organization focused on
Black Liberation.
A religion
That worships a
brown man lynched
by Rome.
A special hello,
friend.

Petty greetings and a hearty fuck you:
to every church
that passed on me because I was too
radical
Queer

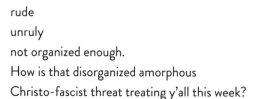

rude
unruly
not organized enough.
How is that disorganized amorphous
Christo-fascist threat treating y'all this week?

This stanza is dedicated to:
every person who pretended they
didn't see
hear
believe
I existed

as sat on the sidewalks
from Market Street outside
the gallery mall

to sidewalks
on Market Street outside
the Warfield Theatre

and every Market Street and marketplace
in between
as I said,
"Can you spare some
change to get something to…"

Juicy is so carved into the archways
and tall soaring edifices

that is now hip-hop
lore, history,
and martyrdom
that it's hard to see
the song for what it was
when it
dropped
August 9 of 1994.

Juicy is the hip-hop song your mom knows.
Tell her I said what's up by the way.

It's like the only one a white person knew right
away when they bought this book. Think about it.
They might not have known it was called "Juicy."
But they know the beat, they know the samples,
they know all the Diddy parts. We see hip-hop
as the unstoppable entity in media—TV, fashion,
social media, commercials, and titans of industry
all have embraced this art, because it crossed the
magic line of avant garde street poetry occasion-
ally allowed in CBGB's and some unknown Black
places, spaces, doorways where new music was
born. Places most of Manhattan never would have
hung. With downtown Julie Brown shoving a mic in

Bobbito's face as Stretch was using a handheld recorder to try to catch the RZA, an unknown, at a Junior Black Mafia show with Lil' Cease. That's how the media worked, some MTV VJ like Julie interviewing real heads in the scene like Stretch and Bobbito who had a midnight college station show. My "cousin" would drive to NYC to record every weekend off the radio, and we would hustle the tapes the next week. I mean two hours of hip-hop gold in the middle of hip-hop's golden age. That's what "Juicy" is. Christopher Wallace is the only Christopher I acknowledge in history. Biggie was the most gentle soul I ever saw from the era caught on camera at times with his guard down. I know it's strange to say, his music was wild, incredibly enticing and hypnotic. *Ready to Die* as a whole album had the soaring heights and beauty and raw liberation that emanated from the average kid I grew up with. Everybody I grew up with was a hero. Sorry not sorry. White america and sometimes my own community won't acknowledge that. By hero I mean like Nephilim.[1] Which had all the problems of a young Black man in the concrete jungle at the time.

It's hard to understand what ready to die meant
to first:
Bedford-Stuyvesant
(Salute to Bed-Stuy forever)
Then
Brooklyn
(Salute to "the world")[2]
Then
the rest of us...

This chapter is dedicated to:
Every cat who ever sold me
a bootleg
tape, CD,
blasted some real new hot shit.
(Salute) to the blocks of Fifty-Second Street
between
Market Street and Walnut in West Philadelphia.
I mean "Juicy" is so
carved into the archways and tall, soaring edifices
that is now hip-hop lore, history,
and martyrdom
that even in the moment
the here and now of then and there
you could feel it all the way in the wastelands

of NYC's Angry AF little stepbrother
through an arranged marriage set up by capitalism
that moved the Emerald City
from parents of the nation
to a poor working-class mess full of
brawlers, ballers, the end of Heuy P. Newton
TSOP[3]
The city of Philos.
In Philly,
the few times
I stopped through or
vagabond past in my "escape from the hood"
I'm embarrassed I ever thought I could outrun
Blackness as a teen,
that my little brother told me about the album
over the phone
Where was I?
Wyomny?
I embarrassed I bought bootlegs of every
seminal hip-hop
album
as a kid.
As a kid with twenty bucks
for the month,

what are you going to do?
Walk into a Tower Records?
Thank you, brave merchants of the subversive,
first to hand me a Kufi, Marcus Garvey's words,
not a teaching moment
but a moment
where I first encountered poor righteous teachers
For handing me "Juicy."
Because that's where my brother copped it
Put it on my radar
(Salute) To the merchants of Fifty-Second Street
who point constantly toward the way of peace.

This line is dedicated to the Fugees who said:
Islam your land, Islam my land.

Machine gun funk cut through
all that,
one clip, two clips
gimme the loot, gimme the loot,
I mean how the fuck could I not
fantasize after

MOVE
Gimme the loot

After MOVE
Gimme the loot america
Before you burn my whole block down.
After the MOVE incident
Which incidentally, like its forebear,
Tulsa, OK,
was completely legal
state-sponsored
terrorism.
The MOVE "bombings"
Made me want to drop bombs.

        What is the strategy of MOVE?
"The strategy of John Africa"
And what's the
strategy of
John Africa ...?
"The strategy of M.O.V.E."
............................You're not telling me much about
your plans
Shit that reporters say.
"I'm not telling you my strategy"
Shit that freedom fighters say.

Why would I tell you, Officer Wilson Goode,
I mean, Mayor,
I mean, Officer Al Sharpton,
I mean, reverend,
I mean, op.
I mean I want to fit in so
when should I pull up my pants, Bill Cosby?
After you get off parole or Megan's list?

I mean what else can be said about the only
Christopher we acknowledge?
You think Christopher Columbus means shit to
anyone who was treated like cargo?
White culture doesn't think about the fact that we
were sentient property

Think about it.
Nor does it *think*
about the thought *construct* of
ownership
objectively.

I think Christopher Wallace,
I think Christopher Wallace
I think Biggie Smalls

changed hip-hop
as a side note on his way to change
america's collective consciousness
and its perception
of you
me.

I think Christopher Wallace
changed the cosmos
the fabric of reality.
truly.

How are we even talking right now?

How does this book exist?
Will it truly exist or will the industry

make me dumb it down
for white people to catch
every cultural reference
for their own inspection like the vultures they be?

This conversation we are having across
time and space
maybe there are
multiple versions of reality

where this book may or may not
exist.
Art exists in every life I believe.
Every world,
forms, shapes, dances, rhythms remember from
life to life.
Art is the chosen dialect of
the universe. Divinity likes to speak in song.

Jesus. Love. Allah. Olodumare. Mother Earth.
Sophia. The Lady.
The living interconnected being that births
the raw multiplicity that just is
the natural universe
COSMOS.
Humanity's defender
pulling us

whipping us,
cajoling us,
inviting and
demanding that we join those moving the great
juggernaut.

Humanity
and those who stand in balance

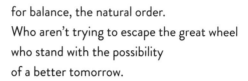

for balance, the natural order.
Who aren't trying to escape the great wheel
who stand with the possibility
of a better tomorrow.

What will white america do
when no longer it is just HISstory?

I recognize that we are just returned friends
singing songs we once knew to almost family
I mean familiar people
in a familiar world
facing a familiar threat:
our collective
inability
to be in harmony with
one
another may lead to more than political instability.

What I'm saying is I had a dream once
that all the universe is a series of songs
which are each part of just
one
song

more a chorus
more like angels, messengers, trickster, prophets,
and the seers
all dancing around one singular point
soothing, loving, and midwifing us all
into being.

What I'm saying is that we can see small cracks
into that reality.
They spill into our world and walk around
and they make music.
I have seen a few of them in person.
From Garcia, to Ebo Taylor, to
Junior Mafia.
The throne of Christopher Wallace
Aeon, which in hermetic teachings means
Great s/hero of past worlds and stories
returned.

I think we didn't recognize Christopher
and recognition is not
fame, money, contracts.
It isn't masks, or distractions, or
recognition.

Being recognized in this world means no matter
the corner

mosque, open mic, pulpit, palace,
or executive office, and
white houses built on Black bodies
in blood red–stained lands,
The world stops

and says simply: I see and I hear you.
I see and hear you, Christopher.
It was all a dream.

Thirteen

Out on the Streets

"Out on the streets
(Yeah)
Where I grew up
(Ah, hah)
First thing they teach us
Not to give a fuck
That type of thinkin' can't get you nowhere"

—The Roots, "How I Got Over"

You who denies the
Son of
Man if you only knew

out on the streets
where I grew up
first thing they teach you is to not give
in.
To not betray who you thought you were going to
be
with who you are
because that is all you think is possible.

I was baptized in
Harold Melvin and the Blue Notes,
I grew up knowing more stylistics songs
than Bible verses,
I can tell you why my daddy loved, I mean
unabashedly *loved*
Hall and Oates
so much that he unilaterally adopted them into
Black peoples.

He would sign the adoption papers around
midnight every
other Saturday night after enough E&J Brandy
that Blue Magic and Dee Dee Sharp shared
the same opinion

and were on their way to cosign.
Who was I to argue with that?

If you aren't rooted in TSOP,[1] then you probably
won't see how I make the claim The Square Roots,
The Roots Crew, are the best thing Philly has
birthed into hip-hop.

I can hear the schooly D[2]
Crate digging
scholars who know the real
birthplace of gangster rap
check me about "P.S.K. (What Does It Mean?)"[3]

Well "Betcha" by Golly Wow[4]
I'm glad that you brought
up the seeds
that led to the tree
that gave us dope fruit
like Meek, like Freeway, like
state property.

Impossible tasks 1.0
taking the whole unwashed, uncouth,
and unbothered
mass of Philly in they arms

in an ever-widening embrace
while holistically, esoterically,
radically, politically, telling truth,
to a beat, a rhythm, sixteen bars, and
Black music alive.

With not a slouch in the crew
I present the Roots.
I present the album How I Got Over
With its twin
Undun.
Both will
undo your ass.

Illadelph Halflife[5]
showed us the Organix.[6]
We smoked that back home.
Think I got it at King Bosh.[7]

When we were asked "Do You Want More?"[8]
What else could we say?
Yes.
Yeah man I'll cop two of those
jawns. Them jawns[9]
right over there.

You see right over there
on two street
down the street from the bar
where a bunch of seditionist landowners
decide they wanted the bounties
of this land as their own.

I mean if you took a nice carriage
ride through "Historic Colonial Philadelphia"
after the Liberty Bell, and where those Dear
Gentlemen
did some light treason there on Second Street
in the back room of the Second Street tavern
where you can still see historic period
servers.

I mean if you were some dopey midwestern
whose historical understanding never crept past
middle school in a carriage
the frauds, copies, and other fakes we lay out for
tourists because you and your fucking militia
cousin been trying to steal the declaration since
the '80s you inbred fuck on this block where there
more bars

than any other square block radius in america is
another bar where slaveholding fucks listen to an
inventor.
Slave-dressed folks still work there so you can jerk
off later at the Holiday Inn while this one sleeps.

You see right over there they declared
independence,
around the corner from Franklin's place.
Before you get to Champions Steaks
make a left.
That lil alley jawn is where it happened:
the first place I saw The Square Roots
who became The Roots.

I didn't know you could play bass and drop
into a solo supported by your rhythm guitar
while the horn section punctuates every
line, rhyme, sixteen bars, Amir was saying that day
or even attempt
to complete the unbroken chain

from the crossroads where Esu Odara[10]
and Robert Johnson first cooked up the scheme
of earthly immortality

and hiding his Black and blues-filled tired soul
in his music,

from the living spark
the flames of

Little Richard Queer Divine Being.
From Ebo Taylor to Harold Melvin
to Pigmeat Mcgraw,[11] the one thing
that lost poets have in common
is they are rooted in the history, lineage, beauty,
and utter gift of
this Black music.

Black art
Black thinking
Black thought is perhaps one of the best MCs
ever.
Full stop.

Dear God 2.0 is the best sixteen bars about existence from
a sidewalk-up
perspective.
An El stop–down perspective

in the grand story
Of the MC's quest for Love.

What can you say about Questlove?
What can you say other than thank you?
Thank you for making my love of music
not a senseless meander into cultural artifacts not
my own.

When I finally let The Roots into my life, I was
so frustrated with how my peers looked at music.
I hated how anything that was rock and roll was
"white boy" music when I knew for a fact that it
was ours. We had shaped it, invented it, birthed it,
and watched as the record industry had to create
a whole separate billboard chart to keep us from
dominating the top. How the name Little Richard
brought out derision, or how with a living, breath-
ing Prince walking around, they weren't interested. That Sam Cooke was thrown in the dump-
ster with Bad Brains. I remember the first time
I saw Fishbone and the whole crowd was white
except me and the band's homies. Shit wears on
you honestly.

Maybe it was the way a white girl stepped on my new sneaks on my way to see P-Funk the first time or the sad look on Charles Bradley's face as he crooned out the most soulful shit ever to drop from the Orun[12] to pale white faces in an endless sea of media-driven hits and premanufactured stars.

But somewhere between the time my daddy took me to listen to the Ohio Players behind the Mann Theatre fence—where all the locals in the know sat and listened to every band for free—and the time I saw The Roots, I had lost hope in emergent live music not just coming out of just two turntables and mic or live bands being a major part of hip-hop. It just seemed like the natural progression of the DJ and the MC was basically them on stage with Earth, Wind & Fire and a couple white boys from Chicago (the band, not the city, but from the city).

Enter The Roots.

They felt like something had finally escaped from the industry's prison of

you are way too highbrow and intellectual for
today's market
can you throw some rims on that shit
or
be confined to a
coffee shop neosoul world of slam poetry and
B songs written for nary a straight person, even
though they loved them.

I mean nobody was thinking about Thelonious
Monk set to breakbeats, or so I thought.
Then I watched a tuba player stage dive.
Then I watched a guitar solo set to some of my
favorite verses.
Then I looked around and realized this was all
happening in my hometown.

I fell in love with The Roots that day
Because it was clear The Roots loved me
enough to believe that I was just a smart a fan
as they were musicians, that my history mattered
to me
as much as it did to them.

The Roots were the first time hip-hop respected
someone

like me, the artist raised in almost twenty-plus
years of hip-hop culture
who didn't have anything novel, new, or unique to
say
but saw hip-hop as a medium to tell a really
old story, in an old tongue, to a new world.

The Roots where the first band
I noticed in hip-hop to tip their hats
to the oldest idea in art.

None of this shit is ours.
It has roots that run deeper and further back
than *my* story, *my* ideas, or anything *any* of us
come up with.
We are but a thread in a grand tapestry
retelling a story that was never ours to begin with.

Fourteen

I'm Gonna Buy the Bus for You, Mother

"Ah-ha, hush that fuss
Everybody move to the back of the bus
Do you wanna bump and slump wit' us?
We the type of people make the club get crunk, say
Ah-ha, hush that fuss
Everybody move to the back of the bus
Do you wanna bump and slump wit' us?
We the type of people make the club get crunk"

—OutKast, "Rosa Parks"

Does it matter that the name
Rosa Parks meant Crunk

to more kids I knew at the time
than say the Bus Boycott?

Does it matter that Organized Noize[1]
was more exciting to me as a teen than
organizing at the time,
and that I would prefer to be
Dungeon Family[2] rather than the SLC one.

Does it matter that Rosa was chosen from the
secretary pool
because the woman who punched
that same driver in his face
and the pregnant teen he threw off weren't good
"strategy"?

Does it matter that Black people can be so
strategically manufactured by our own
in an attempt to be acceptable in *they* white home
we are re-created, reformed, and rendered in
their mind
as light enough, well-spoken enough.

Articulate in the unlettered language
of those inarticulate in the language of the heart

how does one articulate that white perception is a weaponized language?

What does the respectability politics of this new phraseology prove or disprove

other than: Oppression?

By the time OutKast hit the scene, it didn't matter to me in any really discernible way if they were manufactured by the industry to be the "next" thing in its anthroposophical approach to music. By this time, watching early MTV interviews with hip-hop artists by white "veejays" was like listening to Darwin interview Fred Hampton.

> Darwin: So you live in these environs here? Where the air quality seems to be subpar, the homes are substandard at best, education and access to services is threadbare at best, under the constant threat of death in your own community because [*pauses to check field notes*] of a textile industry and religious law that just recently stopped [*checks notes*] one

hundred years ago after a very significant resistance politically that led to years of bloodshed, is this correct?

Informant one [*only goes by "Big Boi" and appears to be a local seer or oracle*]: Well yeah we grew up here, and a lot of us hung out here in the Dungeon Family basement, you know it was [NAME REDACTED BY CAPITALISM] house and his mom's just believed in us.

Informant one smiles as we look around the conditions they are forced to work under in the new regime that has arisen since their "Civil War" most seem unaware that nothing has really changed or how poor their conditions are, will send notes to education workers and aid teams.

Darwin: Great, and the machine you have over there, where you and your tribe simulate your ancestors' tribal drum sounds from Africana?

Informant two [*only goes by "Andre 3000" and seems to be some sort of fertility priest who also uses the rhyming oral epistemology so common among the unlettered darker peoples*]: Yo what the fuck you—

Darwin: [*I interrupt informant two's attempt to dominate me, it's best with these tribal leaders to remain in control or they will start to recount their tale of woe to you again.*]

Follow up. Can you explain why you go back to this superstition when you live in one of the most civilized countries in the world?

Cut to Kurt fucking Loder.
Or at least that's how every early hip-hop interviewer looked to me.
The surprise on a New Yorker's face
when they realized that the South wasn't all cotton fields and mother fuckers singing "Wade in the Water"?
You think Bushwick Bill and the Ghetto Boys'

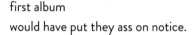

first album
would have put they ass on notice.

It doesn't matter to me if OutKast was
manufactured,
or at least, subverted by
the industry's encouragement for hip-hop to get
into its Party and Bullshit
stage á la the Last Poets' song "When the
Revolution Comes."

In the same way it doesn't matter to me
if Rosa Parks was a strategic asset
deployed by the NAACP and the SLC
to ratchet up things for the Bus Boycott.

The result was freedom
Or at least a glimpse of it.
By the time
OutKast dropped the song "Rosa Parks"
it didn't matter to me
there was nary a reference to this sainted leader,
other than let's party back there now,
because that was the point of the song.

What's it matter you can ride on the front of the
bus
to your shitty dead-end capitalist job.
Like your father.
Like your grandfather.
To end up paying a city out to kill you taxes.
Retake the back of the bus.

What's it matter if they gave you Gucci links
icegrills, chains made of children's sweat blood
diamonds.
Fuck Jacob the jeweler when it comes to our
liberty.

Your mama ain't stay up all night
and with your granny dreaming about what you
would be
to end up another fucking shelved product, what
the fuck man we came here as
cargo.

What's it matter if you are a product
when most of us don't even know we are for sale
like we even do this shit?
Why should you keep riding this dead-end

bus?
Why even sit back here with not enough to eat,
pay rent, survive
and still create?

Maybe my great-grandaddy
maybe my great-granmamma
maybe saw all this coming and created me
so I could create art, so you could create art.
That way the back of the bus

becomes the place to be
children of the Diaspora
make anywhere we at
the place to be.

Make they lily white consciousnesses
of they children
pay to get in.
That's right, Richard,
Little Johnny *paid* to get in here.

That's right your genteel Georgia Bulldog,
polite and poised suburban Tennessee Volunteer ass
kids are all walking around talking about some
hey daddy:

Ah-ha, hush that fuss
Everybody move to the back of the bus
Do you wanna bump and slump wit' us?
We the type of people make the club get crunk, say,
Ah-ha, hush that fuss
Everybody move to the back of the bus
Do you wanna bump and slump wit' us?
We the type of people make the club get crunk

I think the one mistake that white supremacy made is
believing
respectability couldn't be weaponized.

One of my most grievous errors when reviewing the histories of my ancestors was
believing
respectability couldn't be weaponized.

SLC and others used respectability, Western pedagogical models, ontological constructs, political instability, literary criticism, decolonial counter-narratives, and theological imagination to create new possibilities for Black peoples.

OutKast, Organized Noize, Geto Boys, the entire Dungeon Fam, and others:

Used respectability, Western pedagogical models, ontological constructs, political instability, literary criticism, decolonial counternarratives, and theological imagination to create new possibilities for Black peoples.

We don't see it that way.
When we discuss wordplay
double meaning that has triple meaning
lines beaming with historical reference
cultural advances sent across the airwaves

That only those who are initiated in Black culture invited to the cookout
got a hood pass, actually have Black friends, etc.
so forth and therewith.

Can you hear how many citations
are needed for the average hip-hop
song to be translated
before it can really be critiqued?

That's why I don't pay much attention to the reviews

or what the average listener says
or what Tipper Gore says.
O'Reilly you only riling me up[3]
I never gave a flying fuck
what the authorities said about hip-hop.

The Christian Bible has
become a cultural
time bomb
ticking away
in lil Dante's head.

Hip-hop is a cultural
time bomb
ticking away
in lil Johnny's head.

Might as well:
move to the back of the bus
do you wanna bump and slump wit' us?
we the type of people make the club get crunk

Assata Shakur

Fifteen

Why Do We Steal So Many Songs from Assata?

"In the Spirit of God
In the Spirit of the Ancestors
In the Spirit of the Black Panthers
In the Spirit of Assata Shakur
We make this movement towards freedom
For all those who have been oppressed, and all those
in the struggle"

—Common, "A Song for Assata"

A bunch of times in my time
trying to move along with

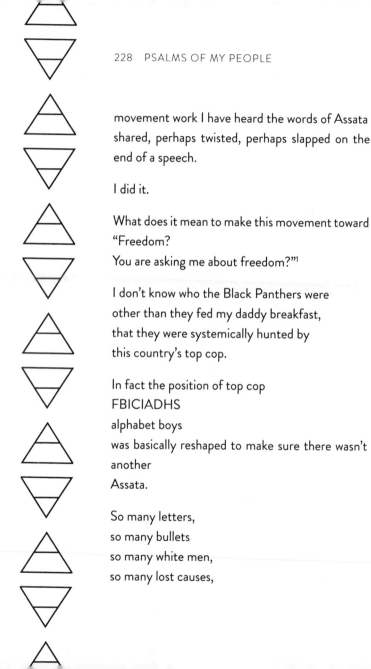

movement work I have heard the words of Assata
shared, perhaps twisted, perhaps slapped on the
end of a speech.

I did it.

What does it mean to make this movement toward
"Freedom?
You are asking me about freedom?"[1]

I don't know who the Black Panthers were
other than they fed my daddy breakfast,
that they were systemically hunted by
this country's top cop.

In fact the position of top cop
FBICIADHS
alphabet boys
was basically reshaped to make sure there wasn't
another
Assata.

So many letters,
so many bullets
so many white men,
so many lost causes,

so many words that
one could say
but really Common
said it all:

"I met this girl when I was ten years old
And what I loved most, she had so much soul
She was old school when I was just a shorty
Never knew throughout my life she would be
there for me
On the regular, not a church girl, she was
secular"[2]

It's common in hip-hop
to speak of all hip-hop as a monolith.
Not a Divine Feminine
objectively speaking it is strange
how many light-skinned mutherfuckers like me
Like to speak for "her."

This book wants to trouble the waters
problematize the glittery downloadable
and completely self-contained insta
instant-celebrity package that hip-hop has become.

But I refuse to lionize her elders
or the systems of oppression that it is
always going to be entangled in
like we are caught in the entanglement
that is this empire.

I am just saying it's common
to put words
in Black women's mouth.
be they poetic indulgence, Orisha, organizer,
or your mama. I'm guilty.

I was born AMAB.
"Male" for those of you who don't leave home
a lot.
My entire brain is me singing scat versions of
what Black women taught me
and to pretend otherwise is arrogance.

It's common in the movement
to hear people bring up
Assata as an example
although I doubt
they know what it means
to actually go toe to toe
with the State and not the internet.

We started this exploration,
car wreck,
piece of written
prima
material culture,
anti-intellectual,
antiproperty,
anticapitalist artifact,
by talking ancestors.

We end there,
where nothing ends.
In the ancestral realm,
trying to honor
a Messenger of old
returned.

If you are the Mother Moses
of your block,
the one the kids
flock to when the world
does what this wicked world does
to Black children

like Assata
You are the product of your ancestors.

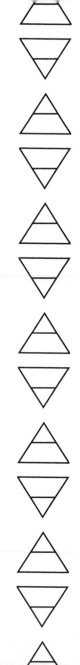

The next link in the chain
of stories, an oral epistemology.
The secrets of civilization itself
all descending through time
and ascending history
to make her the wildest dreams
of her ancestors.
Assata is a product of her ancestors,
you are the next link in the chain
of stories, an oral epistemology
the secrets of civilization itself
all descending through time
and ascending history
to make you the wildest dreams
of your ancestors.

Like Assata
you ain't the first
of your blood
to have the blood,
to just be
absolutely constitutionally incapable
of being a traitor

to those who are in chains

under the yoke of the red, white, and blue
which is made by mixing the
Black, Brown, White, and Red
and
bright Yellow

of the splintered medicine wheel,
A sacred hoop on a turtle's island
we should never have known
burned in the bowels of this nation
stolen fucking land.

And to the prisoner,
those of us who are draped,
in colors like
Red, Black, and Green,
With no Black Star Line[3] home,

well we are supposed to be just
so fucking grateful
that the cage is more
comfy.
Better bed, cable, a timeline feed,
less chokeholds, opportunity
and a cold war since 1865

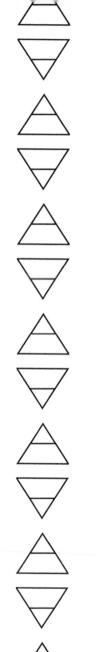

just don't
rebel.

A lot can happen to you on your own like that.
Hanging on a limb way past where things are
supposed to be ...

What was the air like in the hours
before Assata Shakur was
born into this world?
Was it electric,
like could you feel
the latent kinetic energy
about to explode?

Was the moment of Assata's
first scream out of little lungs
is it those same child cries
the same ones
that
was heard
throughout the cosmos?

Or were those to come later?

Assatta Shakur is a clarion call

an unveiling
or in Koine Greek
an Apocalypse.
She undressed this empire,
charged with forcing the
nubile, uncorrupted minds of
young americans to gaze upon the
naked visage of this land of milk and honey.

Assata is guilty
of calling us over to examine
the wrecked husk of an age.
To look at the grand colossus we call this
world, construct, paradox, riddle
surrounded by
conundrums of colonialism
and yet as angry as I am for being awake.
I am so angered by the awareness she brings forth

I can't imagine a world without Assata
I wish I lived in a world that didn't need Assata.
Not the one we know.
I wish I knew her.

"Freedom?

You are asking me about freedom?"[4]

Like a doctor
examining the body of a long-dead
idea
in an exam room in the college of London
1834,
she starts to tell you what ails this
thing that had the nerve
to masquerade as your home.

Imagine:
you can hear her now describe what her
apprentices found,
the disease that has killed our world
or futures, choking our hope
that we all now have.

Imagine if the dead body
of the american dream could talk back:

"Soon after I was born,
gentlemen,
I fell into these maladies
under which I now labor.

My face is fresh and ruddy
because people have petered it and colored it
with lakes; my sickness resembles the ebbing and
flowing of the sea,
which always contains the same water,
though it rises and falls,
with this variation notwithstanding,
that when my looks are outwardly good,
my malady is more grievous inwardly
(as at this present), thus,
when my face looks ill,
I am best within.

As for the infirmities which torment me,
do but take off this gay jacket,
wherewith some good people have covered a
rotten carcass,
and view me naked
as I was made by Nature."[5]

america hates to be stripped bare
in front of everyone.
All eyes bearing down on its
scars, and metastasized cancerous heart.

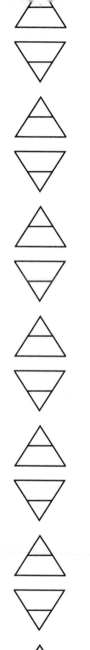

The machines, tubes, wires,
and ventilator because running through its barely
moving
body
is white supremacy.
That's the only science america accepts.
That's the only calculus whose results america
believes in.
america accepts freedom when it has no
other choice.

But there Assata was
coldly assessing the course of the sickness.
How deep it ran.
Looking down on the patient
and deciding that it would be better
to lose a limb,
than
the whole body.
The whole people.

What must it have been like
to be fully sentient
alive and aware

that you were the embodiment of
generations behind you
in front of you
with the whole world hanging by a thread …

and to be left
with nothing
but a sidearm.
A permanent rabbit
on your jacket.[6]
A child they want to assassinate
in your womb.
Beaten, tortured,
in what you called
a new form of plantation

Only here would we
sentence the wise surgeon
the skillful healer
the one ready to face this contagion
and pox
to exile.

An empire's …
last,

gasping,
breath ...
can ...
take
decades.

Assata Shakur is John
(John should be so lucky)
Cuba is Patmos
(Patmos should be so lucky)
and this is the end
of apocalypse.

The death of death
and these old stories
Assata is Sophia
the Mary who after walking a long road
stands now draped in Black
a Black Madonna
machete in hand.

You are the Alchemist,
and there are plenty of sugar cane
fields to burn.
Actual plantations

still completely
intact and ready for you
to dismantle
deconstruct

or

maybe just a really fucking cute wedding
OMG.

Like this one advertises
Literally at the time of writing:

> "Experience/Professionalism and <u>True
> Southern</u> Hospitality Belle Grove Plan-
> tation tastefully blends the advantages
> of modern day services with the charm
> of authentic **Old South** surroundings to
> provide you and your guests a memorable
> occasion."[7]

The last
Kingdom (Oyo) within the society of
kingdoms

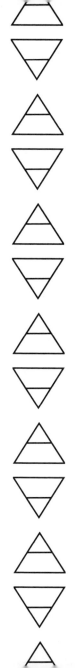

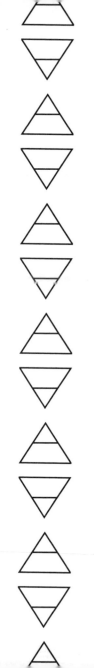

Or what we now call
nations
that my ancestors came
from did not fall until
1940.
"White" folks (a new creation)
had been looking for us again since the time
of Nero.
As a political concept, construct, and to create a
new term for terror, rape, and land theft.
Real estate. A term and new legal concept coined
by the family and then the young scion
of Virginia planters: I mean we know who is really
planting the cotton[8]
as a
badge
of honor
you lucked into
as a never-ending well of unseen social credit and
capital.

It's strange when
whiteness discovers something.
In the early
nineteenth century we were

stumbled upon
by a group of really
sharp "explorers"
who thought the Niger River ran
the opposite way.
We should have ran the
opposite way.
But we had,
my ancestors
had resisted
the Ottoman's
great empire
as whispered from
Otura as Imole[9]
to my ear.

That's one people group
        What about your ancestors?

In the Spirit of God
In the Spirit of the Ancestors
In the Spirit of the Black Panthers
In the Spirit of Assata Shakur
We make this movement towards freedom

For all those who have been oppressed,
and all those in the struggle

—Common

Aboru Aboye Àbósíse![10]
Assata Olugbala Shakur[11]
Olugbala
Iba se[12]
Olugbala
Iba se
Olugbala
Iba se
Olugbala
Iba se
the Olugbala escaped!
Iba se
Olugbala still lives!
Iba se
Olugbala burns in your heart!
Iba se
Asé,[13] asé, asé![14]

Afterword

"Penmue-Theosis"

I have attempted in all my time as a writer to bring you real-time reporting from my inner landscape. I have never once pretended that the interior universe of my heart was not: full of ideas, some of them ugly, raw, and reaching for life, desperately trying to germinate in my mind. I believe in this way I am honest.

Truly, I hope that I have transgressed your purity, taken away your sense of safety, and added warts to the face of not just the church but also this wicked land.

I hope that I have brought you from within the murky and often glitter-filled depths of those strange interior environs some of what I see as beauty, hope, joy, and love as I understand *her. I knew her before Christ; I am so grateful she never let me go.*

In the final analysis, the Jesus I once knew is no more.
We need new stories, new myths, and new scripture.

This same Jesus I believed fervently would drag out into the world for us liberation, a new expansive realm of kinship and joy that Jesus is long dead in the american consciousness. I now believe the church to be an enemy of that particular "Jesus's" very resurrection.
america just wails "what would you have of me child of the most high" and the radical Jesus who came from outside of history, into history, looks sadly back.
I wish him better luck getting through to the people in the next world his consciousness visits.

Being an "anointed one" seems like a shit gig.

I honestly feel bad for a "Jesus" who fills oppressed sexual and gender minorities, Queer trans folk, full of terror. I was a pastor. Now when I hear someone just "sharing the Gospel of Jesus Christ" to a stranger on the street I want to fucking throw up. That message is a mockery of what Jesus preached, taught, or was.

Being a pastor was a shit gig, to be honest.
The church is full of really good people, and institutions make sure they keep those people near its most vital organs. Lest we lash out. Lest we cut our ties to it. Lest we slay the dragon, the serpent that waits on the edges of night.

The current state of the american mainline church—in particular, liberal thought and the liberal arts' staunch defenders, the sacred keepers of the postreformation knowledge—is a funhouse mirror of itself. It is an anathema even to the *scraps* of truth the church has allowed to dribble out over the years. Centuries. Two millennia. Haven't we given "the church" enough time? Every age, the church swears it will repent of its sins and that at the dawn of THIS century, like every century before since its birth, it now sees how it's been literally destroying the world as we know it.

Again.

I am unsure of the effect of my movement work or its long-term impact. If my ancestors are right, and this is all just a cycle of stories playing out over and over again, then what is politics? Won't nature take its course? Are we just another tiny voice stepped on on the road to pax americana?

I tire of the cycle of america's grievous wounds. I tire of pouring out poetry, art, theology, ontology, and truth on her already parched and rather ugly throat. I tire of preaching either to those who know, and refuse to get up, or to those who have not the skills to listen.

I never tire of writing, of art, of the secret craft brought to us by Penemue in the book of Enoch.

> "The name of the fourth is Penemue: he discovered to the children of men bitterness and sweetness;

And pointed out to them every secret of their wisdom.

He taught men to understand writing, and the use of ink and paper.

Therefore numerous have been those who have gone astray from every period of the world, even to this day.

For men were not born for this, thus with pen and with ink to confirm their faith;

Since they were not created, except that, like the angels, they might remain righteous and pure.

Nor would death, which destroys everything, have effected them;

But by this their knowledge they perish, and by this also its power consumes them."
Book of Enoch 68:9–16.

This is a book about the power of poetry to transcend time and space, to be added to rhythms so we can project our very selves to other points in history. What you hold in your hands is a piece of my soul that could not be cut but had to be slowly gnawed off me by the process of creation. While writing this book, I was also a PhD student at the Graduate Theological Union trying to put together what I call "a people's history of magic." For brevity's sake, and proposing a new form of magic, what I am calling *Penemue-theosis*.

The building into the very structures of writing, art, adornment, charm, wonder, and allure in either performed or crafted moments and artifacts as magic. Art is magic. Poetry is magic. The performance is magic. The experience of receiving art is magic—the act of drinking in with all the senses something an artist crafts, fully experiencing another's work. Those moments when they were alone in the dark rewriting, repainting, reassessing, refocusing, replaying, and recounting the stories of the Divine. Art is the act of becoming as close to the Creator as possible or becoming like unto our holy parent. The deification of art, artist, and audience. Or a less heretical framing: all three are drawn so close to the presence of the Creator to everyone else it looks like Divinity has come to earth.

It is only the truly lost who care which is which. Only the truly bitter hearted would witness miracles and demand to know what doctrine it is from. As part of an early experiment of this new form of magic, the idea of this book came to me.

Not Penemue-theosis.
This word would return to me later.
But the idea that we of this time and place needed holy words. New stories. New ways of expressing what we already know. Deep down inside.
Psalms of My People is a small piece of this larger idea.
The need for psalms sung by those who still worked the fields, tended the sheep, or just wandered the land. Where was the scripture for those who died last week, last year, or just the last generation? While at the time it seemed like a "novel" idea for me to do it with hip-hop, to use the way you remembered the song to take you back to the "feel" the energy, or Ase, of that time. But this is, in my opinion, all I ever did from the pulpit or in previous books. This is the essence of art.

I think I have failed at this quite miserably, but every artist does at the end of great big endeavors. I have successfully avoided the trap of creating another didactic book about the history of hip-hop or some tell-all memoir-ish piece about my beef with artists whose talents I can't touch. Full stop.

I also didn't hide the cognitive dissonance that I used male, homophobic, and problematic artists as a Black Queer trans artist. I wanted to use materials similar to biblical scholars and others who study sacred text, where the parts you have to use to tell a story are often deadly to you, the storyteller. I am not sure if this is an attempt to redeem these artists of my youth or to rediscover them.

What can I say? This book is a love note to teen lenny. You should write yourself love notes so bold that others find pieces of themselves reflected in you. But tend to those wounded parts of you as an artist beloved, come hell or high water. It's not your job to sell what you create. We create because we must.

This love note is written to little lenny; before he knew he could use "they," he struggled with his identity around gender, sexuality, and how he was othered among the others. I had known all my life that gender felt like a game, an act, a dance, a mask. *Particularly masculinity*. It would be years, escaping an incredibly abusive situation at home fueled by homophobia in part, and moments like this where you stand up for your art and who you are in print. Win, lose, or draw, I believe whatever art is, it favors the bold. He also fucking loved hip-hop music or, at least, his encounters with it. That is also objectively true, and without any nuance, he would have picked every one of these songs. That shapes the form of this book.

I have left those moments of uncomfortability intact, in the same way the soaring heights these songs took me to are left mostly intact. *Because I still struggle with this.*

I am still willing to struggle for hip-hop culture, even if I might not be willing to struggle for the church. I enjoy wrestling with Eazy-E more than wrestling with Benedict or some papal bull or the latest thought leader's new book about how we can save the church in three easy steps.

Or with any organization's movement leaders, for that matter. I no longer find life in much else but art.

In art there is resistance, there is love, there is joy, there is life, and a Creator beckoning still.
In art I find a sentient form of magic crafted from our deep wells of collective consciousness.
In art I found a home.

Remember it is better to serve humanity than ideals. Remember that justice doesn't last nearly as long as people. Remember you're the record-keeper for this age, for this time, for these people. Drink it all in, whole.

Dear artist, and by artist
I mean sorcerers
Tell the story.
Tell them who won't listen or relent in their hate.
Tell them who we are, what wonders we have wrought, and why we are here.

"One is not attempting to save twenty-two million people. One is attempting to save *an entire country, and that means an entire civilization, and the price for that is high. The price for that is to understand oneself. The price for that, for example, is to*

recognize that most of us, white and black, have arrived at a point where we do not know what to tell our children. Most of us have arrived at a point where we still believe and insist on and act on the principle, which is no longer valid, that this is such and such an optimum, that our choice is the lesser of two evils, and this is no longer true. Gonorrhea is not preferable to syphilis.

The time has come, it seems to me, to recognize that the framework in which we operate weighs on us too heavily to be borne and is about to kill us. It is time to ask very hard questions and to take very rude positions. And no matter at what price."

—James Baldwin, "The Artist's Struggle for Integrity"

Acknowledgments

Lisa Kloskin. We fucking rule.
Lester Wrecksie. We love.
Ash the mystic I write this in hopes of Texas sunsets
with you.
The princess of the fields: two acknowledgments in one life!
Don't tell Penelope.
Lightfoot. Are we having fun yet?

Notes

Chapter One

1   James Baldwin, "The Artist's Struggle for Integrity," New York City Community Church, November 29, 1962.

2   Baldwin, "The Artist's Struggle for Integrity."

3   Ase: Yoruba for "make it so," but it also is the living connective tissue and energetic web that moves through all things in creation. It is the energy or the force that is the proof of the Creator's radical immanence, meaning the Divine exists in all matter.

4   John Africa was the founder of MOVE, an anticivilization, antitechnology, earth-based philosophy that was birthed by Black peoples in West Philly. It became an intergenerational

and diverse movement. Through a series of Cointelpro-style attacks in the 1980s, the remaining members of MOVE were harassed and activated to the point that they saw anyone who approached as an enemy. When I was a kid, they moved their headquarters to six blocks from my house and were "loud" and "disturbing" to neighbors. To counter the complaints of neighbors, tired of being attacked by the city and the police, and now a decade later, members of MOVE who had joined the campaign unwittingly set up loudspeakers on the roof. In response, the Philadelphia Police Department immediately orchestrated a stand-off "to protect the neighborhood" and then dropped explosives on their roof. The police ordered the Fire Department to stand down and burned my whole neighborhood down on the south side of Market almost from Osage Avenue on. True story.

5   See Ferguson, Missouri, Consent Decree and Department of Justice findings in the wake of the Mike Brown uprisings. Mike Brown forever.

6   Meaning and meaning making. Remember kids, the academy is all smoke and mirrors.

7   If you don't think Trayvon Martin was lynched and murdered, or can't at least see how I could say that, do yourself a favor. Put this book down, beloved. Once you look into the abyss, it looks back. It will find you as wanting as me. Abandon all hope who pass these gates.

8   Yoruba for "destiny."

9   UNESCO, Intangible Heritage, "Safeguarding Our Living Heritage," accessed March 1, 2023, https://ich.unesco.org/en/.

10 Worringer and Nealman are two white cis men I have known who have arguably known more about hip-hop, what the newest hottest track was, where to cop all the best drops for sneaks, or graffiti culture than I ever could. These cats, in their own way like Charles 13X, the founder of the 5 percent movement, were inspired by and encouraged others to more actively engage in the five pillars of hip-hop—Charles Nealman particularly for me at a point when I was "fed up with hip-hop," an event that happens like Saturn's return every few years with the right alignment of the stars and bullshit in my life. I loved live music and festivals; this led to more Antibalas, Charles Bradley, jam bands, and

clones of jam bands but a lot less hip-hop. Dude would put me on to a new album all the time.

11   Brian Coleman, *Check the Technique: Liner Notes for Hip-Hop Junkies* (New York: Villard, 2005); Kathy Iandoli, *God Save the Queens: The Essential History of Women in Hip-Hop* (New York: Dey Street Books, 2019); Christine Otten, *The Last Poets*, trans. Jonathan Reeder (New York: World Editions, 2004); Neil Kulkarni, *The Periodic Table of Hip Hop* (New York: Ebury, 2015).

12   Only deceased family members. There should be no pictures of the living, except pictures of yourself alongside the deceased.

13   Ifá is an Indigenous practice of modern-day Nigeria, and the main philosophical, political, spiritual or esoteric, scientific, cultural practice of over 75 percent of enslaved African peoples of the last fifty years of chattel slavery, making it almost half of Black America's "ancestral," or indigenous, practice.

14   Originally *his*; changed by the author for a more inclusive reading.

15   Wande Abimbọla, "Introduction." in *Ifá: An Exposition of Ifá Literary Corpus* (New York: Athelia Henrietta Press, 1997), 43.

Chapter Two

1   Modern-day Lagos, Nigeria. Traditional Osun Territory.

2   5150 ENT., "Rare L A Riots Footage Easy E and Mc Ren Interview 1992," YouTube, accessed March 1, 2023, https://www.youtube.com/watch?v=brKBPfc0mU0.

3   Yoruba term for the creator. One translation is the Womb of the Cosmos or Universe.

Chapter Three

1   Valcahi was the first person to go on record to the federal government about the Mafia. He is also what Loretta Mary Burndette Sweeny Duncan, my sainted mother, called any child who told on the behavior of another. "You little stool pigeon, go get you Valachi papers then." Use in a sentence, "Heard the came out with his Valachi papers, that's why they dropped the charges."

2   List compiled by Renée Ater, accessed March 1, 2023, https://www.reneeater.com/on-monuments-blog/tag/list+of+unarmed+black+people+killed+by+police.

3   An incomplete, not in complete chronological
     order, list of slain hip-hop artist since 1987.

Chapter Four

1   Rick Ross, or "Freeway Ricky," is famous for a
     drug empire built in the '80s during the height
     of the crack era. Sentenced to life in prison at
     one point but now free, he has his own biog-
     raphy out, so you can read his version. Ricky
     has long been considered a missing piece in the
     Iran-Contra Affair, in which cocaine and weap-
     ons flowed from the united states to South
     American countries to empower cartels and
     destabilize the local government, and one of the
     consequences was the proliferation of cocaine
     in America—so much so that it required a
     cheaper version to support the growing version.
     Urban legend says, enter Freeway Ricky and
     the CIA and add the LA drug scene, and crack
     is invented.

Chapter Five

1   In case you have you haven't guessed, this poem
     is about DJ Kool Herc, the person credited

with discovering the "break" or the "merry-go-round," which consisted of looping two records that were at the same beats per minute at the "break" or long jam in the third section of most popular funk, soul, and disco records. For DJ Kool Herc, it was James Brown's third section repeated with "Bong Rock" by the incredible Bongo Band. This party in the Bronx is hip-hop's birth. The MC, or master of ceremonies, at the time was more an announcer who tried to make announcements at the party fit in with the flow of the music. DJ Kool Herc became obsessed with this idea in Jamaica, where he was from, watching "selectas" or Reggae and early Dub DJs. One can catch an "ode" to this in the third section of Boogie Down Productions' "South Bronx."

2   Jamaican slang for a DJ in the reggae, dub, and soul and funk style of the island and the forebear of the hip-hop DJ.

Chapter Six

1   Nasir Jones, or NAS.
2   The last two albums from Nas as of writing are *King's Disease* volumes 1 and 2. "King's disease"

was a folk name for gout, a disease one can only have from "not having to move," according to Black culture. A disease brought on by decadent eating, living, and laziness.

3   A Hoodoo title similar to what white practitioners of esoterica, magic, witchcraft, or sorcery would call Master or Mistress. For very obvious reasons in the Reconstruction period, *Conjure and Hoodoo* practitioners used the term *doctor* instead. Originating in Black culture where our people who applied "prescriptions" similar to the African notion of "eboo" in Ifá—thus, Doctor. Eboo, although vulgarly translated by colonizers and their eager helpers in the Yoruba kingdoms as "sacrifice," I believe is more rightly understood as a combination of three words in English to really be grasped, and all three must be held in one's mind at once. It is the combination of the words *sacrifice*, *prescription*, and *tradition*. Sacrifice in the sense of effort: we sacrifice time, energy, etc., to go on a journey either of self or spirit, for example. In Ifá, this is the practitioner seeking the Awo or Olorishate. The effort to go ask an elder, "What should I do?" Prescription in the sense of what the Awo

or Olirishate says is the "eboo," for example, two thousand cowries, shea butter, and fun (a chalklike substance). This is based on tradition; the Awo or Olirishate "prescribes" the eboo based on Ese Ifá verse or an oral epistemology of approximately, at minimum, 1,200 memorized poems, proverbs, or koans even. These stories indicate eboo, carrying a lesson in Ipa Pwele (good character) and always a sacrifice. Either to thank the Orisha, the Creator, or other traditional spirits.

Chapter Seven

1   A phrase first used by the incredible Black Thought of The Roots crew. Arguably the best MC to come out of Philadelphia.

2   James Baldwin, *The Cross of Redemption: Uncollected Writings*, ed. Randall Kenan (New York: Vintage Books, 2010), 55.

3   *Use your Google machine* before you fact check me. Clown: Dianna Theadora Kenny, "Music to Die For: How Genre Affects Popular Musicians' Life Expectancy," The Conversation, March 22, 2015, accessed March 1, 2023,

https://theconversation.com/music-to-die
-for-how-genre-affects-popular-musicians
-life-expectancy-36660. They did science and
mathematics. You in the footnotes on some
emotional shit. These cats did that for you.
They made it a tribute: "List of Murdered Hip
Hop Musicians," Raptology, accessed March 1,
2023, https://raptology.com/list-of-murdered
-hip-hop-musicians/. Why are you really check-
ing this citation? Why would Black people lie?
While you are looking things up, look up *phony*
in the dictionary.

4   Baldwin, *Cross of Redemption*, 55.
5   Baldwin, *Cross of Redemption*, 55.
6   Baldwin, *Cross of Redemption*, 56.

Chapter Eight

1   The CIA experimented with LSD in the early
'60s to create Manchurian candidates in other
countries. Ken Kesey, Terry Nichols, Timothy
Leary, and even Bill Wilson of AA fame all were
participants and had their lives changed irrevo-
cably by their involvement.

Chapter Nine

1   Nadine Frederique, "COINTELPRO," Encyclopedia Britannica, December 17, 2018, accessed March 1, 2023, https://www.britannica.com/topic/COINTELPRO.

2   *Overstanding* is a word that is a counternarrative language-building example and a play on *understanding*. Who wants to stand under whiteness's language? Better to weaponize it. Its roots are in Rastafarianism and the Garvey movement; it is embedded in hip-hop language to accentuate a Black perspective elevated above the understandings, definitions, and ontology given to us by whiteness. This decolonial vernacular embedded in American language and pop culture allows Black folks to have their own language within their colonizers' language. *You call that shit slang.*

Chapter Ten

1   Go listen. Why do I gotta point everything out? Magna Carta fam. Listening to music is implied in a book about music.

2   *Ire*, often translated as "good fortune" or "luck," really is more like the concept of being "on path" or following a mapped path to a chosen destination. The destination being one's Ori, or chosen destiny at birth.

3   The Holy Prophet Muhammed's (may peace and blessings be upon him) wife, legendary for her dedication to her husband and being his confidante, friend, and early supporter of his ministry.

4   Peace and blessings be upon him, or PBUH, is usually to denote the Prophet Muhammed (PBUH) in the Quran. I am extending that denotation not to make a comment on the Islamic traditions that span the globe but to denote who Malcolm is to Black peoples here.

5   Pick 12 means: *pick twelve jurors we are going to trial*. An actual threat against the State, kids, not your "rights." Pro-tip out there, freedom fighters: if you ever find yourself locked up in the prison plantation system, can't afford bail, but are being offered the worst deals ever, first of all welcome to america. I'll be your host, lenny. Your rights, the truth, what should happen is never a factor in the "justice" system.

The factors are money, population of jail, and severity of threat to community, which simply just means will you make headlines if we let you out? The average full jury trial for the State is about $50K to start. There isn't a lot that is worth that much to the State, including you. Word of warning, don't actually go to trial dumbass: *you can't win*. Just threaten it up until the end; you most likely will walk with time served. Is your crime worth that much to the State is the question, not your innocence. If you don't make it convenient, you may have a shot. Buy me dinner when you get out, fam.

Chapter Eleven

1   A *hotep* is a pseudo-intellectual, typically a cis, heterosexual, Black male-bodied person who always tries to use the tools of the master to prove that they are free. They often create fantastical theories around scripture or migration patterns or use the well-known critiques the academy has of itself, and the colonial project, which themselves are typically led by Black women intellectuals, whose work a

hotep typically barely understands when they use them uncited. These cats will tell you that ancient Egyptians were aliens, a very old white supremacist lie that brown people couldn't build the pyramids (too primitive), but then use that same idea to prove Black peoples are descended from Divinity and thus should be the true rulers of the earth, which should look exactly like white culture: men in charge, meek quiet woman, Queer niggas like me dead—you know the vision because it's white america 2.0 with just your weird ass uncle in charge. You will spot them by their kufi but no deen, chewing licorice root, but they can't tell you the Odu it comes from; then they tell you they own ancestral stuff is witchcraft, how Jesus from Palestine was Black from the Congo, how a print from Ghana, they swear, is from Nigeria. Maybe they selling you a book directly because "the white man" (which for real might be real, but also they books usually be wild AF, like worse than alchemy grimoires from Renaissance Europe for context) or a CD that is baffling as all hell, and they are typically dressed with so many mismatched culturals from the Diaspora on their adornment and clothing they look like Fifty-Second Street in Philly threw up.

2   The Three Initiates. *The Kybalion: A Study of the Hermetic Philosophy of Ancient Egypt and Greece* (Chicago: Yogi Publication Society, 1936).

3   Baldwin, "Struggle for the Artist's Integrity."

4   Sacred bird of the Yoruba people, the assistant to the Spirit of the Lagoon to some. Sacred to the "Mothers."

5   In the Holy Qur'an: the people, or the people of Allah (God), or the people of Islam (the way of peace).

Chapter Twelve

1   Hebrew for "giants," a reference to angels who came and lived on earth, had children, and were divided into those who could remain and those who were destroyed in the flood of the Hebrew Bible.

2   This is '90s slang for Brooklyn borough. There are cats who make Brooklyn their world and claim they have never left. Never even to go to

Manhattan. It is based on the belief that all
you would ever need is present in your community. Or some shit Tribe Called Quest said
once.

3   The Sound of Philadelphia. It's a historical Black
recording studio and record label. It is also the
title of the *Soul Train* theme, it's a culture, it's
a mostly ignored large part of Black music history. It's a thing in other words.

Chapter Thirteen

1   The Sound of Philadelphia. It's a historical Black
recording studio and record label. It is also the
title of the *Soul Train* theme, it's a culture, it's
a mostly ignored large part of Black music history. It's a thing in other words.

2   Early Philly hip-hop artists credited by Ice T,
former members of NWA, and others in the
LA hip-hop scene, as the first gangsta rap, or
the first single they heard that had the raw visceral feel of the streets that they were experiencing. It talked about the hustler lifestyle and
what it took to just make it through a day in
the hood that was more reflective of the lived

experience of a young generation coming of age at the advent of the crack era. This makes South Philly the birthplace of gangsta rap and gives Freeway, Meek Mill, and others a more direct lineage to that music.

3   "Park Side Killers," the name of the independent single released by Schooly D in 1985 credited as the first gangsta rap. I mean literally. In the singular since it's the first single. Bye. Get back to the book weirdo, I know my shit.

4   Very popular hit by the Stylistics, a seminal member of TSOP. You should listen to them now.

5   The Roots's third album.

6   The Roots's first album.

7   Famous bodega in West Philly from the '90s.

8   The Roots's second album and first live.

9   Philly slang word that can replace any noun. For example, hand me that jawn over there. Or, check out that jawn over there. Or, this jawn in my hand.

10   Divine Messenger of Transformation. The Trickster at the Crossroads. An Orisha that is known and honored in various ways in several African Traditional, and Diasporic African Traditional

belief systems. Mistaken for the devil by early missionaries, it is my belief that this is who Robert Johnson met at the crossroads and not the adversary from the Christian Bible.

11 First recorded hip-hop song according to some hip-hop heads. It was in the slam poetry style, or bare-bones of hip-hop. "Here Comes the Judge," recorded in 1968, is considered more hip-hop than other Black poets at the time.

12 Yoruba word that means "home." Often translated by colonizers as "heaven."

Chapter Fourteen

1 Arguably the best production team and label ever, but certainly a contender for the crown in the South.

2 Production team, label, and crew that gave us OutKast. Famous for launching out of their homie's basement.

3 Jay-Z, "Threats," *Black Album*.

Chapter Fifteen

1 Quote from a phone interview with Asatta Shakur included on the track "Song for Assata," Common.

2   From "I Used to Love H.E.R." by Common, on his 1994 album *Resurrection*.

3   Name of the shipping company owned by Marcus Garvey.

4   Quote from a phone interview with Asatta Shakur included on the track "Song for Assata," Common.

5   Arthur Edward Waite, *The Real History of the Rosicrucians* (New Orleans: Cornerstone, 2008), 62.

6   *Rabbit on your jacket* is an out-of-use old-timer or long-term sentence holder, slang from prison. It means you run. Either at the moment of arrest, or you have escaped a facility, or you have escaped custody, prison, or you just fall off the map when on probation or parole. I am the rare one who has been charged with all of the above, with the escape occurring from a minimum-security juvenile facility in the months leading up to my eighteenth birthday. I mean yes, every charge I ever received was for marijuana. But I have never peacefully gone along with my own arrest. I mean really who does that? As soon as I hear the sound the State bracelets (handcuffs) make, my first instinct is to swing; isn't yours? Incidentally they could keep you until you were in your mid-twenties

in the juvenile system. My plan was shit, and I ended up in one of Colorado's finest "boot camps" in a juvenile state prison. They were all the rage in the '90s.

7   Belle Grove Plantation, events web page, accessed March 1, 2023, https://www.belle groveplantation.com/events.

8   Obviously a play on the line from the first Cabinet Battle in the Broadway Musical Hamilton. See also, for reference, the Beastie Boys song "Rhymin and Stealin" from License to Ill.

9   A way of talking about the oral corpus of Otura, one of the Odus of Ese Ifá verse, or the Yoruba way of life called Ifá. It's the thirteenth "book" of Ifá, Ifá being one of the names of Spirit of Destiny, Orunmila, whom those who receive "Awo," or the secret, meaning the corpus of stories, divination tools, training, and initiation, are dedicated to in the Yoruba tradition. The "book" of Otura deals a lot with the Ottoman invasions and colonizing, whether this is an addition, or not tradition received by all, it is well documented that at least since the thirteenth century the "Muslim in White Cloth" has been a recurring character in Otura Odu.

10   "May prayers and offerings from the market-place be raised back home." Personal transliteration of common Yoruba greeting and prayers phrase.

11   She who struggles, a Savior, the Thankful One. This is not the meaning of Assata's name. This is Assata's name in English.

12   Yoruba "for we give praise."

13   "May it be so" in Yoruba. Also refers to the energizing force of the universe.

14   A short Ese Ifá verse composed by lenny duncan.